THE
MILLIONAIRE MAKER

Praise for *The Millionaire Maker*

"Loral is the real deal . . . she actually makes millionaires."
— T. HARV EKER, author, *NY Times* #1 best seller,
Secrets of the Millionaire Mind

"Read The Millionaire Maker *and create the wealth of your dreams today."*
— MARK VICTOR HANSEN, co-author, *Cracking the*
Millionaire Code and *The One Minute Millionaire*

"Loral Langemeier's engrossing new book, The Millionaire Maker, *has a very simple goal: to make you a millionaire. After all, that's what Loral does for a living. I recommend anything that Loral writes, but most of all, this warm, readable, eye-opening book."*
— JAY CONRAD LEVINSON,
author of the Guerrilla Marketing series

"I personally know countless people who are millionaires today and credit Loral with their financial success. Read this book and become a member of Loral's millionaires' club!"
— BOB PROCTOR, author of *You Were Born Rich*

"The Millionaire Maker shows you how to quickly take control of your financial future and achieve all your dreams."
— BRIAN TRACY, author of *Getting Rich*
Your Own Way, Million Dollar Habits,
and *The Psychology of Selling*

"With the financial makeovers performed in The Millionaire Maker *you'll find 12 new building blocks to create your own wealth."*
— CHET HOLMES, CEO Chet Holmes International

THE
MILLIONAIRE MAKER

Act, Think, and Make Money
the Way the Wealthy Do

Loral Langemeier

McGraw-Hill

New York   Chicago   San Francisco
Lisbon   London   Madrid   Mexico City   Milan
New Delhi   San Juan   Seoul   Singapore
Sydney   Toronto

The McGraw-Hill Companies

2 3 4 5 6 7 8 9 0   DOC/DOC   0 9 8 7 6

ISBN 0-07-146615-0

FIRST EDITION

This publication is designed to provide accurate and authoritative information
in regard to the subject matter covered. It is sold with the understanding that
neither the author nor the publisher is engaged in rendering legal, accounting, or
other professional service. If legal advice or other expert assistance is required, the
services of a competent professional person should be sought.

> —*From a Declaration of Principles jointly adopted by a Committee*
> *of the American Bar Association and a Committee of Publishers*

McGraw-Hill books are available at special quantity discounts to use as premiums
and sales promotions, or for use in corporate training programs. For more information, please write to the Director of Special Sales, Professional Publishing, McGraw-
Hill, Two Penn Plaza, New York, NY 10121-2298. Or contact your local bookstore.

Cash Machine, Financial Filing Cabinet, Financial Freedom Day, Freedom Day,
Gap Analysis, Wealth Account Priority Payment (WAPP), and Wealth Cycle
are trademarks of Choice Performance, Inc.

Interior design by Arlene Lee

Library of Congress Cataloging-in-Publication Data

Langemeier, Loral.
   The millionaire maker : act, think, and make money
the way the wealthy do / by Loral Langemeier.
        p.   cm.
   1. Finance, Personal.   I. Title.
   HG179.L264   2006
   332.024'01—dc22   2005022032

This book is printed on recycled, acid-free paper containing a
minimum of 50% recycled de-inked fiber.

To Dianne,
*you left this planet much too soon. Your
presence still resonates through everything we
do and the memory of your humor, kindness,
brilliance, and grace guide us forward.
Thank you for your extraordinary impact
and all you gave to Live Out Loud, Logan, and me.*

To Logan,
you are truly the gold at the end of all my rainbows.

Contents

ACKNOWLEDGMENTS

To write a book like this takes a lot of support and encouragement and I want to thank all the amazing people who surround my life. Of course, to include everyone who has cheered on this effort would take too many pages, but I'd like to thank a few.

Thank you to everyone at McGraw-Hill who helped put this together. Jeanne Glasser, thank you for your vision and for finding me. Thank you to Mary Glenn, Lynda Luppino, Jeffrey Krames, and Philip Ruppel for your support and for being on the edge of your seats when I showed you your first Gap Analyses. Thank you also to Caroline Sherman, for doing what you do, and the PR and marketing firms for their great efforts.

I am very grateful to every member of our Live Out Loud community, including members of Loral's Big Table, who have trusted me to mentor and coach them on their various routes to millions.

They've shared their stories and their dreams, and together we've made them one and the same.

Thank you to the wonderful team that works with me every day to create Team Made Millionaires, including Jay Pearson, our recovering financial planner and IRA guru; Sue Walker, with whom I share coffee and discuss saving people from financial distress every day; Fred Auzenne, our cactus king who can make any old widget look exciting, as long as it's got a great ROI; Wendy Byford, whose knowledge of entities has been invaluable; Ken Starks, our mortgage broker who's opened up his world to include the exciting ideas coming from our team; Paul Rogers, the best land-buying firefighter I have ever met; and Steve Parker, who is the epitome of a great team player.

Thank you to my many terrific field partners, whom I know will be helping me create a lot of wealth for a lot of people for many years to come.

Thank you to the great Live Out Loud Coaches, who help our clients reach their Freedom Days every day.

I'm very grateful to have Mark Myerderk on my team; his bigger, better brain and capacity for all things lawyerly has kept me sane.

I so appreciate the home team at Live Out Loud and in remote locations around the world. Your support and team effort have been and continue to be invaluable to our success.

Lots of thank yous to my mentors, Bob Proctor, Jay Conrad Levinson, Sandy Botkin, Chet Holmes, Robert Kiyosaki, Mark Victor Hansen, and Brian Tracy, who have taught me innumerable lessons and invaluable skills.

Big thanks to Jay P., Wendy B., Lori W., Joni K., Sue W., David Z., Steve P., Jennifer M., Mark M., Fred A., Aaryn H., and Gary H. for putting your eyes on this book, guiding me forward, and reining me in.

Thank you to my Mom and Dad and my siblings, Jeff, Doug, Kent, and Holly, who saw me through those endless mornings of walking the beans and gave me the courage to walk west and sow my own harvest.

I owe more gratitude than I can ever express to my Aunt Bev, who gave me the confidence to just say yes and figure it all out later.

A very special thanks to my California family, Shea S., Jim N., Serene C., and, of course, Clare and Tim B., who have supported my life's work by helping care for my son and having such a significant impact on his life.

And the biggest thank you of all to my son, Logan, first and foremost in my life, for sharing his vivid imagination, healthy perspective, and unconditional love for me and this spectacular life we're living.

—Loral Langemeier

INTRODUCTION

I was on my way out of the office when the television producer called. "Loral," she said. "We want to do financial makeovers."

"Sounds good," I said. I put on my headset and went to my car. The sun was still high over the hills of Marin County, just north of San Francisco. I figured I could get a bike ride in with my son Logan before dinner.

"But we have a problem," she said.

"What's the problem?"

"Well, we want to do a series of TV segments throughout the year, where we take a family and help them build wealth."

"That sounds good," I said.

"Did you hear what I said?"

"You want to help them build wealth."

"Right, we don't want to tell them how to build wealth. We actually want to *build* their wealth. On TV," the producer said.

"And?"

"And, you haven't hung up on me."

"Should I?" I asked.

"Well, we've talked to a few well-known wealth builders and asked them to do the show. And they told us that they could work with people on their perspectives about money and their behaviors, but that they aren't comfortable assuring us that they can actually make people wealthy on TV."

"That sounds like the reason I came into this field in the first place."

"Do you think you can do it?" the producer asked.

"I know I can take anyone, anywhere, and make him or her wealthy."

She laughed.

I didn't.

She cleared her throat. "Really?"

"Really."

I make millionaires. It's that simple. I have a straightforward, strategic approach to creating wealth. The key to my approach is a proprietary system I created several years ago called the Wealth Cycle Process, which is a method of generating cash through assets and income. In this wealth-building process, your money truly works for you. Even if you start out with a great deal of debt, once you set the Wealth Cycle Process in motion, you can be on your way to having everything you ever wanted much faster than you ever thought possible. The truth of how to build wealth has been known forever, but most wealthy people have never taken the time to share this information. By understanding how the wealthy make money, you can too.

I was not born with money or connections. I grew up on a farm in Nebraska, where I woke up early every morning to do my chores and went to bed early each night so I could wake up early again the next morning to do my chores. From the time I was a kid on the farm to my teenage years I worked hard creating my own businesses; in my early adulthood I worked for a large corporation and juggled my own ventures on the side. I was always pushing myself to create enough money to live the life of my dreams.

And then I figured it out. I discovered the Wealth Cycle, the key to financial success. Now I live the life of my dreams, where money is abundant and I can focus on the things that matter to me: my family, my friends, my health, and my passions. Making money and living a life free of financial concern is doable—for everyone. And because I was brought up to believe that you have to give to get, I took what I learned and created the Wealth Cycle Process.

Too many people think they can't have a lot of money. The fact is

1. You possess every tool you need to make a lot of money.
2. Wealth is about access, and now you can finally access the information and opportunities too long kept in too small a circle.
3. There is no such thing as a self-made millionaire; it takes a team to make those millions.
4. Taking control of your money takes stress and risk out of your life.

The Wealth Cycle Process is a concrete plan. Too many wealth programs are abstract, and that means too many people are learning a lot of interesting, but not very helpful, concepts. Activity, not concepts, will help you take the actual steps toward wealth. Thinking like a wealthy person is good; modeling your behavior after the wealthy is better. The Wealth Cycle is about massive action. My approach, which involves a community of Team-Made Millionaires, supports moving forward with hope and optimism and a belief in our ability to be successful investors. Many other wealth-building programs lose 30 to 40 percent of their clients in the first year, whereas the attrition rate of my coaching programs is less than 1 percent—and it works for people from all walks of life. For example, our Team-Made Millionaire community includes

1. A construction manager who, within eight months of beginning the Wealth Cycle Process, initiated a project from which he would personally earn over $12 million in the next two years

2. A middle-aged woman making a fair salary at a telecommunications company, putting her savings into a 401(k) and hating every day of work, who became an avid student of the Wealth Cycle Process, drove two hours every night to a bread-and-butter real estate market, and within nine months of working with us was a millionaire

3. A receptionist at a law firm making $24,000 a year and spiraling down in debt, who wanted to start her own business and initiated the Wealth Cycle Process with a dog-walking venture that increased her annual salary to $100,000 and pushed her to millionaire status in just a few years

As I said, I make millionaires. It's that simple.

Meanwhile, the television producer asked if I could meet her a few days later in a small town outside of Oakland, California, to tape the first segment. "We're going to roll tape that day, Loral," she said. "Are you sure about this?"

"I'm positive," I said.

But she wasn't. "We have a family of four who are in debt and the mother's about to lose her job. I just want to be clear. You said you're going to get them on the road to wealth in several television segments shot over six months?"

"Yes," I said.

"How would it work?" she asked. I could tell she was nervous about the possibility of having a crew, not to mention an eager family, standing around watching me stand on my head, with no clue what I was doing.

"I will ask them eight questions in eight minutes and come up with a wealth plan for the rest of their lives," I said. "That will be the first segment. Then we'll put the plan in place, and by the end of the series, they'll be on their way to becoming millionaires."

"Loral, our audience has no patience for theory—"

"Neither do I," I said. "The Wealth Cycle Process is not about theory, and I don't present broad strokes that gloss over details. This is a practical approach to becoming wealthy. I will walk this family through the Wealth Cycle Process very specifically."

"But all our viewers need to feel that it can apply to them."

"No problem. You can give me someone who's severely in debt, you can give me a single mom on a low income, you can even give me a guy who's living a big lifestyle on fumes. I can take all of them and make them millionaires. My approach meets them exactly where they are and takes them all the way to a new life."

"Great, maybe I'll do it myself," she said.

"Of course, you will," I said. "I'll see you in a few days."

Getting started just takes getting started . . .

1

THE WEALTH CYCLE
Money in Motion

E ven without winning the lottery, your chances of becoming a millionaire are a lot better than you think. In fact, if you have the desire and conviction to be wealthy, you have a better chance of generating and, more important, sustaining wealth than someone who has won the lottery. This book will take all the mystery out of wealth building. I believe that anyone can take a prescriptive, step-by-step approach to eliminate financial hardship and build wealth of a million dollars or more. And I don't mean just net worth; I mean cash flow—cold, hard cash in your pocket. Those of you who know that cash flow is king understand that I am talking about something real. This book provides that prescription. It's not a magic wand. There are no platitudes or clichés, slaps on the backs or pom-poms. Most wealthy people get that way not by chance, but by taking specific, tangible action. This book is about taking action to generate wealth and make you a millionaire, precisely and methodically.

If I handed you $10,000 right now and you did not understand how to put it into the Wealth Cycle Process, then you would be no closer to generating wealth than you were before you had it. That's because most of us grew up living in a Lifestyle Cycle.

PROFIT AND LOSS STATEMENT

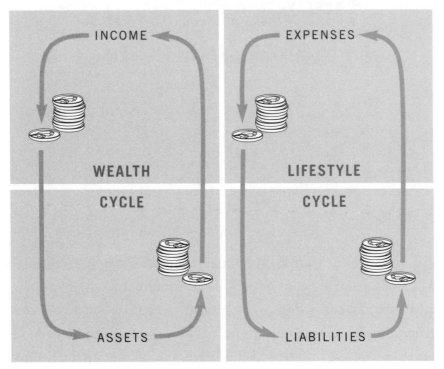

BALANCE SHEET

In the Lifestyle Cycle, wealth can never be built because money that comes in goes right out again to support perishable, one-time-use consumption. And in many Lifestyle Cycles, money is spent, thanks to credit cards, even before it's earned. Conversely, in the Wealth Cycle, money coming in supports assets—that is, money-making resources—that will generate cash flow and create wealth.

The difference between having wealth and not having wealth is the difference between living in a Lifestyle Cycle and living in a Wealth Cycle. A person earning $14,000 a year who understands the concept of a Wealth Cycle has a 100 percent better chance of building and sustaining wealth than a person who makes $1 million a year and lives in a Lifestyle Cycle. And so although it would be nice of me to hand you $10,000, it's better if I teach you about the Wealth Cycle Process.

You Want Passive Income, Not a Passive Life

The Wealth Cycle Process shows you how to continually make money by increasing your assets, thus creating a Cash Machine to feed those assets and steadily building your passive income so you can expand your wealth and live larger. Too many experts tell you to live small, spend nothing, and barely breathe as you dawdle off into the horizon. That sounds just awful to me. I believe it is possible to achieve wealth and have a latte with breakfast. Even if your debt seems utterly daunting, the Wealth Cycle Process will help you spiral your debt down while you spiral your wealth up. That is how the wealthy do it, and it's how you'll do it too. In 1991, when Donald Trump was $900 million in debt, it's pretty clear he didn't shrink his life and focus on reducing his debt. Instead he found a way to rebuild his wealth so that it surpassed and soon eliminated his debt, creating one of the greatest financial turnarounds in history.

While many financial experts are earnest professionals trying to make a living, they can't help the fact that they are commission-oriented and tend to be conservative. Their interest is to keep your money in safe-and-sound accounts. But safe-and-sound accounts aren't so safe and sound anymore. The behavior of a few executives at a handful of companies can cause the entire stock market to swing. Global events, such as terrorism or instability in emerging markets, can cause bonds to sink. Pension funds default, the Social Security system seems shaky, and retirement plans can disappear. These days, all those planning strategies that seemed secure and conservative aren't. Sometimes, putting your financial plan in the hands of someone else is the riskiest thing you can do.

The United States of America was founded on the principles of initiative, resourcefulness, teamwork, and leadership. Abdicating responsibility to a sovereign was shunned, and accountability and opportunity celebrated. Yet less than 7 percent of our population knows how to generate wealth. There was never a class in this, your parents weren't given a special wealth manual to pass down to you, and financial planners have no incentive to teach you what they get paid to do for you. If you make the decision to do for yourself, you create the capacity to be wealthy.

A Year from Now You'll Wish You'd Started Today

You can make the decision to make a lot of money at any age and in any stage of your life. The Wealth Cycle Process will meet you wherever you are. Whether you have a solid net worth and are looking to increase your returns or are deeply in debt, can't forego your day job, and want to be free of money worries once and for all, I will help you become a millionaire, a multimillionaire, and beyond, depending on your personal goal. No matter who and where you are, wealth building is well within your grasp. You just need to step up to the plate.

The 12 Building Blocks of the Wealth Cycle

Just as every person's life is particular to them, so must each person's wealth plan be tailored to the individual. The Wealth Cycle Process is based on 12 building blocks that you will employ in your own fashion, depending on your specific requirements and objectives.

Building Blocks of the Wealth Cycle

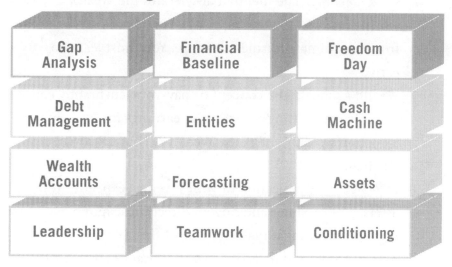

Gap Analysis	Financial Baseline	Freedom Day
Debt Management	Entities	Cash Machine
Wealth Accounts	Forecasting	Assets
Leadership	Teamwork	Conditioning

Each building block is explained in detail throughout this book, but briefly they are defined as follows:

1. **Gap Analysis:** An innovative financial model that will create a map from where you are to where you want to go.
2. **Financial Baseline:** An overview of your current financial situation in the form of a basic profit and loss statement that includes revenue and expenditures and a balance sheet that includes assets and liabilities.

3. **Freedom Day:** The realization of each goal, starting with 120-day objectives and accelerating beyond millionaire status.

4. **Debt Management:** A Five-Step Debt Elimination Plan that erases consumer debt, the greatest barrier to wealth building.

5. **Entities:** The organization of trusts, partnerships, and corporations that hold and service wealth and take advantage of the tax strategies devised by Congress and state legislatures to protect companies and help businesses grow.

6. **Cash Machine:** The fuel that accelerates the Wealth Cycle, which comes from your capacity to create more revenue from a legitimate business venture. You must learn to earn.

7. **Wealth Account:** The concept of pay-yourself-first by consistently committing a portion of earnings for investing, a portion we call *WAPP*, the Wealth Account Priority Payment.

8. **Forecasting:** A projection of your revenue, expenditures, assets, and liabilities and how to direct those numbers into companies that make full use of the tax code.

9. **Assets:** Direct and diversified asset allocation, which is essential to create passive income to feed the Wealth Cycle.

10. **Leadership:** You must learn to "lead your wealth." Though you may, and should, choose to delegate your wealth building, no one can drive the Wealth Cycle Process like you can.

11. **Teamwork:** You must build and direct a team of professionals to help you develop and execute your strategies and reach your goals. Wealth building is a team sport.

12. **Conditioning:** Financial way of thinking. As you accumulate the experience that gets results and gain the confidence

to commit even more significantly to your wealth plan, you will develop a positive and healthy relationship with money.

When you begin the Wealth Cycle Process, you engage each and every building block: they are codependent and indivisible. You will always keep track of a Gap Analysis that will tell you how to get from where you are—your Financial Baseline—to where you want to go—your Financial Freedom Day. You will always employ Debt Management, and if you have or create consumer debt, you will always make it a priority to eliminate it immediately while simultaneously building your wealth. You will always have Entities (legally established companies), which means you'll always run your life like a business. And that means you'll always have a business, a Cash Machine, that will create more money for your Wealth Cycle. You will always run the right expenses through the right Entities, which means you will always be Forecasting. You will always be prioritizing a portion of your money into a Wealth Account used only for investing. And you will always be investing in Assets, and those assets will create more assets, and more and more assets. You will always support these activities with Leadership and Teamwork and be mindful of your financial way of thinking, or Conditioning.

All wealth plans begin with the first three blocks: Gap Analysis, Financial Baseline, and Freedom Day. These three blocks are continuously revised and adjusted throughout the process. Additionally, each person's wealth plan requires the bottom three foundational blocks: Leadership, Teamwork, and Conditioning. The middle building blocks, though engaged simultaneously, are used in different sequences and with different emphasis, depending on the needs and wants of the individual wealth builder. Proper sequencing is essential to the Wealth Cycle Process.

The Right Thing at the Right Time

The most common mistake I see in wealth building is people doing the right thing but at the wrong time: for example, paying down all existing debt before beginning to build wealth. In the Wealth Cycle Process, you begin the Five-Step Debt Elimination Plan and *simultaneously* create a Wealth Account that starts generating wealth for you.

I also see people maximizing their 401(k) payment and holding all the equity in their house. As you'll come to see, this is the wrong thing at the wrong time. In our sequence, you jump right into direct asset allocation. Other wealth advisors might call this irresponsible, but I believe you need as much cash available as you can pull together so you can invest now and start building wealth right away. Those who advise that you live in fear and maximize your money in qualified plans are actually hindering your efforts to accumulate wealth and build a millionaire plan.

Doing the right thing at the right time, namely, *sequencing,* is the foundation of the Wealth Cycle Process. This book will help you understand which building block sequence is right for you. The examples used throughout are selected from the thousands of people I've helped make millionaires and specifically highlight particular building blocks, as well as reflect the entire range of possible sequences. More important, at least one of the examples featured will mirror your own financial realities and goals. My hope is that the next time you and your friends are sitting around a dinner table, you'll be able to identify one another with one of these types, for example, "Oh, you are so Rick Noonan, you'd better start looking at your assets."

In every case we start with a Gap Analysis and the eight questions: (1) What is your monthly income? (2) What are your monthly expenditures? (3) What assets do you have? (4) What are your liabilities? (5) What else? (6) What do you want? (7) What skills do you use to make money? (8) Are you willing to create and execute the Wealth Cycle Process?

From these questions, we sequence the 12 building blocks of the Wealth Cycle. You'll examine this process through the stories of seven different people, each representing seven different routes to wealth. We start with the Leonard family members, who were threatened by a job loss and wanted to generate more income. Their case provides us with an introduction to the entire process and an overall look at each of the building blocks.

In each of the subsequent chapters, we show a different sequence and emphasize a different building block. For example, the Assets building block is brought into focus through the case of Rick Noonan, who made a good living but had several underperforming investments. The Cash Machine is explained in the discussion of Patricia Beasley, a single mother who started her own Web design firm. Kerry Kingsley, a business owner who was not retaining much of the revenue she brought in, portrays the need for Entities, and Forecasting is represented by Jim Quinlin, a victim of taxable money. The importance of the Wealth Account and the Wealth Account Priority Payment are clarified through the opulent lifestyle of Jean and John Jones, and math teacher Chuck Wallace's scenario sheds light on Debt Management.

You Don't Have to Be Ready—Just Go

After you've read through the examples, you will better understand sequencing and choose the right path for your specific needs. In fact, you'll probably start to anticipate your own sequence as you read through the examples in each chapter. But if by the time you're finished with this book you're still unsure of your personal sequence, I will connect you with one of my strategists for a free half-hour telephone session. The contact information is listed in the Resources section at the back of this book.

Getting Started

Wealth building is a dynamic, continuous process that consistently engages each building block. While some of the building blocks of the Wealth Cycle Process are more fun and exciting than others, they are all critical *and doable*. I know, because I did them by pushing my way past the same mental, emotional, and material stumbling blocks that you will encounter. I was a farm girl who knew it was much better to grow your own tomatoes than buy them, and I knew I had to plant my own seeds. I invested a small amount of money, I took a chance, and I've never given anyone sole power over my money since. The 12 building blocks of the Wealth Cycle give you control over your money and help you establish a lifelong wealth plan.

Eight minutes to a wealth plan for the rest of your life....

2

THE GAP ANALYSIS
Mapping Your Way to Millions

A few days after I spoke to the television producer, I collected some members of my wealth team who are experienced finance and investing coaches and we drove to Oakland, California to meet the Leonard family. As I was getting out of the car, I felt like John Wayne approaching some small town that needed saving. We strode up the walk, ready to face off against the family's financial frustrations and perceived failures.

Mary and Mike Leonard were all that the producer had promised. The couple was smart and dynamic, and they both wanted to start taking their financial situation seriously. Though they had a little bit of savings and a home that had appreciated over the years, they also had credit card debt, a salary that was going away, two sons in high school hoping to go to college, and no plan for their financial future.

After getting to know the family a little, talking to their sons, and seeing their home, I was ready to ask them eight questions that would help them map out a wealth plan they would use for the rest of their lives. I went right to the drawing board to create the schematic for these questions.

This schematic, or map, is the Gap Analysis:

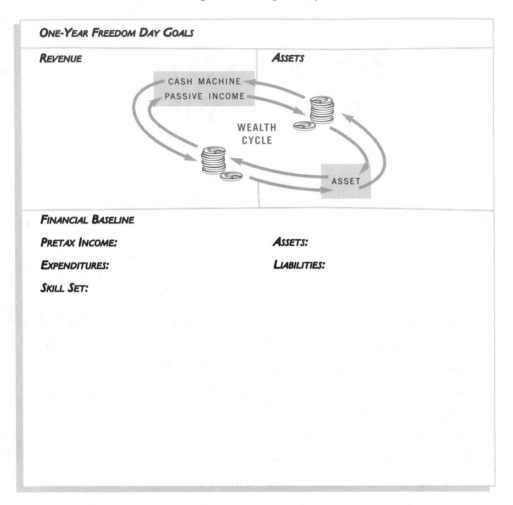

At the bottom is the Financial Baseline—your current financial situation. At the top is the One-Year Freedom Day Goals—where you see yourself in one year. And in the middle we create a Wealth Cycle of assets that will in turn be used to create more and more assets, fed by a constant revenue stream coming from passive income and a Cash Machine.

Mary and Mike Leonard were intrigued but apprehensive. Mary's number one concern was losing her job.

"Losing your job was the best thing that ever happened to you," I said.

"It was?" Mary said. Her eyes scanned mine for a sanity check.

"Yes," I said. "You've been given the gift of urgency."

"That's a gift?" Mike said.

"Didn't you hear me?" Mary said. "I lost my *job*. I need to get another one."

I shook my head. "You are not going back to a job."

"I'm not?"

"No," I said.

She started to cry. Mary had always worked. She'd been brought up to believe that she had to put in 9 to 5, at least, for her money. I could sympathize. I had been similarly conditioned. I grew up in a large midwestern family with very traditional values. Whether I was plucking weeds from the bean field or tending to the cows, sheep, pigs, chickens, or rabbits, I was always reliably, unfailingly, living my myth—the same myth that Mary Leonard lived: work hard for your money.

Given my upbringing, it made a lot of sense that I would think like this. I was born to teenage parents who had little money. As a child, I did not know any wealthy people and I didn't have access to any Ivy League or country club networks. What I *did* have, what was handed down to me from my parents, was a strong work ethic. I started working hard for my money when I was young, helping with the family farm business. At 17, I established a health-training company, and when I was 19 and still in college I created a business that specialized in corporate wellness and human performance. I went on to study and receive various degrees in finance, human performance, exercise physiology, and organizational psychology, and by most measures I had a fairly good career, working for a major oil company, first as an employee and then as a consultant, and then learning my current business of wealth education and mentoring.

I'd always planned to be a millionaire by the time I was 35, but my plan took on a new meaning when I became a single mother. Terrified at the prospect of looming responsibilities, during my pregnancy I decided to put all my efforts into attaining more success in my business, finances, and personal life. And I did it. When I was six months pregnant and just two weeks shy of my thirty-fourth birthday, my net worth passed the million-dollar mark. I had to convince Mary and Mike Leonard that they needed to make this same commitment.

"Boy, is your glass half full," Mike said.

I laughed. "You bet," I said. "There's abundance all around, and I'm shocked how few people take advantage of the opportunity to create wealth." I turned to Mary. "You are not going to get another job."

"I'm not?"

I shook my head. "Most of us want wealth, right?" I said, and Mike and Mary nodded. "But there's activity involved. You don't get to lie on the couch watching TV and eating bonbons and still become a millionaire."

I've never seen real wealth come to those who wait. If you look at many wealthy people, and I'm talking about the ones who are going to keep their wealth for generations, you will see that they are engaged, active human beings. In fact, they're rarely sitting still. I've seen too many people scared of becoming wealthy because they don't want to be responsible for it or "do all that work." And it's true—money takes responsibility and activity. I always tell people, "It's your choice: You can do paperwork or you can be poor."

"We're willing to do the work," Mike said. "We know how to work. But with Mary not having a job and you telling us she's not going to get another one, that seems a bit scary, Loral."

"I bet," I said. "And I also promise that some of the things I'll ask you to do to build wealth will be uncomfortable."

Mary smiled. "Now it really sounds appealing."

Mike nodded. "But, I guess if you're not uncomfortable, you're not growing," he said.

"Exactly," I said. "Given the prospect of the unknown and the requirement of effort, most people choose to stay with what they know and expend less effort. In the short term, it's more comfortable. But in the long run, it's the same old thing over and over: too little income, too many expenses, credit card debt, and no plan for the future."

"That's us," Mike said.

"That's a lot of people," I said. "And it's too bad. Because once a person kick-starts in the direction of a Wealth Cycle, the process has a momentum all its own and the wealth is generated and accelerates faster than you can imagine."

"Sounds good," Mary said.

"It's fabulous," I said. "And every single one of my clients who engages in the Wealth Cycle Process says the same thing. They can't believe they haven't been doing this their entire lives. Not one of them would even consider going back to their old ways."

"I'm in," Mary said.

Mike was a little less certain. "It's not that I don't want to make the effort, Loral," Mike said. "But I don't want to lose anything."

"I don't want you to lose anything either," I said. "Worst thing I ever saw was a 60-year-old man who walked into my office having lost almost everything. He'd worked 35 years as a pilot for one of the major airlines, had trusted his earnings to the airline's pension plan, and lost over a million dollars of savings when the airline announced the default of its pension plan. And people call that security."

Something heavy must have landed on Mike's chest, because he leaned back into the couch with a deep sigh. "I'm not sharing anything new, Mike," I said. "Long before Enron, it was public knowledge that pension plans are not safe or secure. And it's not just pension plans. Look at the mutual fund scandals of 2004. It's not enough that most mutual funds actually underperform the market, but the safe-keeping of those investments has now come into question."

"And what do you think is going to happen with Social Security?" Mary asked.

"Exactly," I said. "Let's look at what security really is. I think wealth building means taking matters into your own hands. At least then you're in control. You know what's going on with your money."

"Can we do that?" Mary said. "I don't know the first thing about investing."

"You can learn," I said. "It's just not that hard, and it's fun. The good news is, getting that knowledge is easier than you think."

The Leonard boys came in from outside and sat down with their parents. It was time to secure a wealth plan for the Leonard family for the rest of their lives.

Eight Questions in Eight Minutes Equals a Lifelong Wealth Plan

Eight questions in eight minutes is the first exercise I conduct with my clients. In fact, at my company's Team-Made Millionaire seminars we often pull someone out of the crowd and do the exercise right there in front of a live audience. Participants learn immediately how to conduct a new conversation about money, because we ask them to share not only their vision but their current financial situation, right down to everything they own and owe, everything they have coming in and flowing out. And then we devise a wealth plan for them.

As you will see from the following exercises, answers tend to be top-of-mind estimates, as do the subsequent wealth plans. When participants leave the seminar, their first step is to uncover their Financial Baseline so they can better understand their current financial situation. When our clients work with us in one-on-one coaching or in our Big Table workshops, they usually come in with their Financial Baselines prepared, so their answers are more detailed. For purposes of this book, we will prepare Gap Analyses for all the case studies the same way we do it at the seminars. Our intention is to show you a pattern of sequencing so you can better understand the building blocks and the Wealth Cycle Process. The examples in the book are drawn from actual scenarios I've had with clients, but they are a fictionalized blend of several real clients. In other words, the names and situations have been changed to protect the innocent. These profiles serve only as examples; none of these case studies or numbers should be viewed as actual investment opportunities.

All the building blocks of the Wealth Cycle are associated with each of the eight questions I ask, but in each question, certain building blocks are emphasized more than others. The important ones have been graphically represented after each question so that you can begin to see how we construct a wealth plan.

Question 1: What Is Your Monthly Income?

The parents looked over at their sons, and I sensed they were not sure about sharing this information. "Money conversations have been taboo too long," I said. "It's time we started having these conversations out loud, so that we can get help, learn, and teach our children about money."

Mary nodded. "I make, or made, $25,000 a year and Mike makes $50,000 a year."

When I ask this question, I'm looking for flat information off tax forms, that is, W-2s for salaried employees or 1099s for those who are self-employed. I also want to know how much their business makes.

In the middle columns of the Gap Analysis we call this *revenue*, not income, because as we create the wealth plan, we will start looking at pretax dollars the way a business does, as revenue—not the way an individual does, as pretax, or gross, income.

In the United States there are two tax systems. One for the poor and uneducated:

Make money ➤ pay taxes ➤ spend money

And one for the wealthy and educated:

Make money ➤ spend money ➤ pay taxes

Americans overpay billions a year on taxes because they don't know how to structure their finances. Forecasting and Entities, two of the building blocks of the Wealth Cycle, focus on tax strategies that will help you retain more of your earnings.

As I showed with the Leonard family, the question "How much money do you make?" causes most people to balk. Many of us have been brought up to believe that conversations about money are in bad taste and that financial success and failures are personal subjects that shouldn't be discussed. As a result, most of us are not knowledgeable about wealth building. This is where the Wealth Cycle Process starts, by talking out loud about money. In fact, the company I built, which is called just that, Live Out Loud, has the purpose of creating a "new conversation about money."

I filled in the bottom of the Gap Analysis with Mary and Mike's answers.

ONE-YEAR FREEDOM DAY GOALS

REVENUE	ASSETS

FINANCIAL BASELINE

PRETAX INCOME: $6,250/month

EXPENDITURES:

SKILL SET:

ASSETS:

LIABILITIES:

- $2,080, Mary's monthly pretax salary
- $4,170, Mike's monthly pretax salary
- No entities, no business, personal bank account

Question 2: What Are Your Monthly Expenditures?

Mary pulled out some papers and her checkbook. "This is our budget," she said. "I think we spend about $3,200 a month."

"First of all, from now on you're going to know exactly how much you spend each month. And second of all, you'll never use a budget again," I said. "This process is not about budgeting and cutting down your life. It's about creating more money to make that life a bigger and better game."

I can't think of a more limiting and unappealing concept than budgeting. A budget is like a diet: no one does it, they don't work, so let's stop it. In the Wealth Cycle Process we do not think about what you *can't* do, which is what budgeting forces you to do, but instead challenge you to deliberately and purposefully plan how you will spend your money. If you want to eat, drink, and be merry, that's fine, but then you need to "learn to earn" more money like millionaires do. "Moving forward, we're going to throw out that budget and introduce you to a spending forecast," I said.

ONE-YEAR FREEDOM DAY GOALS

REVENUE	ASSETS

FINANCIAL BASELINE

PRETAX INCOME: *$6,250/month*   ASSETS:

EXPENDITURES: *$3,200/month*   LIABILITIES:

SKILL SET:

- Manual bookkeeping

Question 3: What Assets Do You Have?

This usually crops up in the form of home equity, mutual funds, individual retirement accounts (IRAs), and savings. The Leonard family's home had appreciated quite a bit since they purchased it, and they had about $350,000 of equity in the house. Additionally, they'd saved money for their boys' education and also had some money in the bank. I could already see the first step in the sequence of their building blocks and knew that to activate the Leonard family's Wealth Cycle, we'd start with the Assets. This would mean taking some of the equity in their home and the money from their IRAs and mutual funds and investing that in more direct, less conventional, assets to create a greater return on their investment. By engaging in direct and diversified asset allocation, we'd wake up these lazy assets and easily replace Mary's income of $25,000 a year.

ONE-YEAR FREEDOM DAY GOALS	
REVENUE	*ASSETS*
FINANCIAL BASELINE	
PRETAX INCOME: $6,250/month	*ASSETS: $397,500*
EXPENDITURES: $3,200/month	*LIABILITIES:*
SKILL SET:	

- $350,000 in equity in their house
- $30,000 in IRAs
- $16,000 in mutual funds for the boys
- $1,500 in cash

Question 4: What Are Your Liabilities?

I'm looking for good and bad debt. Bad debt is consumer debt, usually in the form of credit cards, used to support a lifestyle and not used to build assets. Good debt, usually a mortgage on the house, is leveraged against assets.

ONE-YEAR FREEDOM DAY GOALS

REVENUE	*ASSETS*
FINANCIAL BASELINE	
PRETAX INCOME: $6,250/month	*ASSETS: $397,500*
EXPENDITURES: $3,200/month	*LIABILITIES: $210,000*
SKILL SET:	

- *$10,000 in credit card debt*
- *$200,000 mortgage on the house*

Question 5: What Else?

I continually ask, "What else?" It's amazing how many people take a lot of prodding to truly uncover the real situation and allow us to capture all they bring in and take out—all they own and all they owe. Suddenly, they will say something like, "Oh, I have this stock my grandmother gave me when I was 10," or "I owe my uncle money." This is where we see saving accounts and IRAs come into play, as well as SEPs (Simplified Employee Pension Plans used by small business owners for themselves and their employees), children's educational savings accounts, Social Security income, and even alimony payments. Here also is where all the little orphan 401(k)s show up—you know, the ones left behind at each company you've ever worked for. A business owner I know had 80 employees, but managed over 100 401(k)s on his books; in other words, he had almost two dozen 401(k)s from past employees who'd probably forgotten they were even there. And one couple I know realized, in preparing their Gap Analysis, that they had nine separate 401(k)s from past jobs. The grand total of these nine accounts they'd totally forgotten about was, to their surprise and delight, $109,000. That was a happy day. From this question there are also often side jobs that surface, online auction buying and selling that needs to be accounted for, or other revenue or spending habits that are overlooked.

Mary and Mike looked at their Financial Baseline and shrugged. They had no idea if it was good or bad. I made it clear that I wasn't in the business of judging their situation, nor should they be. Our only concern was where they were going.

ONE-YEAR FREEDOM DAY GOALS

REVENUE	*ASSETS*

FINANCIAL BASELINE

PRETAX INCOME: $6,250/month

EXPENDITURES: $3,200/month

SKILL SET:

ASSETS: $399,500

LIABILITIES: $211,000

- *$2,000 in blue chip stocks from Mary's grandmother*
- *$1,000 owed to an uncle of Mike's with 7% a year interest*

Question 6: What Do You Want?

Now that we knew where the Leonard family was, I asked them where they wanted to go. While Freedom Day represents the light at the end of the tunnel, we want to create an actionable, doable wealth plan that gives results immediately. I often ask clients to come up with 120-day plans that get them toward a year-end goal we call One-Year Freedom Day Goals. The ultimate Freedom Day can be anything you want it to be. For some people, it's as clear as getting out of debt, replacing a salaried job with a more interesting business, and having enough cash flow every month to cover all expenditures. For others, it's a plan to pay for all of their children to go to college or to travel around the world. Or it's a bigger vision, like developing a new product idea or starting a charitable foundation. For many, it's all of these things. And that's fine. But again, to get things started, we're looking for a plan that can be accomplished in the next 12 months. I asked the Leonard family to share their wealth objective. We filled the answers in the top square of the Gap Analysis.

ONE-YEAR FREEDOM DAY GOALS
- *No new job for Mary*
- *Passive income to replace Mary's salary*
- *College tuition plan*
- *Debt elimination plan*
- *Owning and running their own profitable business*

REVENUE	ASSETS
FINANCIAL BASELINE	
PRETAX INCOME: *$6,250/month*	**ASSETS:** *$399,500*
EXPENDITURES: *$3,200/month*	**LIABILITIES:** *$211,000*
SKILL SET:	

In the next two to three years, as the Leonard family moved forward in the Wealth Cycle Process, I could already see what their Freedom Day would include: no job for Mike; a $1 million business; $500,000 of invested assets (that is, the total assets available and used for investment); $6,250 month in passive income; and no bad debt. They could achieve this easily within three years.

Question 7: What Skills Do You Use to Make Money?

"I work for—" Mary said.

But I stopped her. "Whom you work for is interesting, but not helpful, Mary," I said. "Especially since you're leaving there and never going back. I want to know your skills and how you make your money."

"I'm an administrative assistant," Mary said. "Organization, basic administration."

"And?"

"And? And, well, I have good communication and computer skills."

"I'm a mechanic, and I have construction skills," Mike said. "I'm always fixing our houseboat. I built that shed in our backyard. I fix and build things, I guess."

"Like our dune buggies," said Carey Leonard, the older of the two boys.

"They're way cool," his brother, Colin, said.

"Well, yeah," Mike said. "But I mostly fix air conditioning and refrigeration systems."

"Tell me about the dune buggies," I said.

Mike perked up, surprised. Mike, Mary, Carey, and Colin led me to the garage. There were several all-terrain vehicles that seemed to be collecting dust, but in the back was a custom-built dune buggy.

"People freak over dune buggies, and we're like the Jesse James of dune buggies," Colin said, referring to the owner of West Coast Choppers and star of the Discovery Channel's Motorcycle Mania.

"We can build ones way sweeter than what I've seen on the Internet. And those sell for like $20,000" Carey said.

"At least," Colin said. "I've seen some that are $100,000."

"Is that right?" I said. I turned to his parents. "Mary and Mike, it's time to get serious about creating your wealth." I knew with the dune buggies we'd discovered the fuel for the Wealth Cycle.

"This could be your business," I said. "Your Cash Machine."

There are two sources that feed the Wealth Cycle. One is the passive income generated from assets, and the other is the Cash Machine, the business venture. If only passive income from assets circles back into the Wealth Cycle, the Wealth Cycle will not accelerate. It requires multiple streams of revenue, and one of the best sources of that money is a business.

WEALTH CYCLE

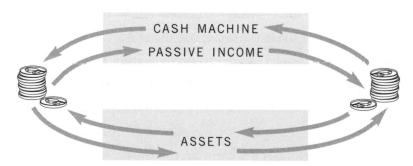

"Well, if I'm going to do my own business," Mary said, "then I want to run a restaurant. Not sell dune buggies."

"Well, you don't get to do that, Mary," I said. "Not yet. Before you get to do what you want, you need to learn to earn."

In creating a Cash Machine, you can set foot on one of two learning curves:

- Entrepreneurship with known skills
- Entrepreneurship with new skills

I don't understand why people would choose the latter when they can nail down the former by creating a business in a familiar field with a skill set they already have, even if it's a less appealing business. This is just a starter business to learn how to earn, and in order to begin its task of feeding the Wealth Cycle, the Cash Machine must generate revenue immediately. The key to finding the right venture is to pick a skill set that you could use to create revenue within a week, even if I pick you up and place you anywhere in the country. That's a Cash Machine.

Later, after you've learned business-building skills in a familiar sector, you can apply them in any arena—in Mary's case, to a restaurant. When I see a person trying to learn how to run a business in an arena in which they have no experience, and with no skill set at their disposal, I'm pretty sure I'll see them quit before they see a penny or learn a thing about entrepreneurship. For those who already have a business, we have to make sure it is in fact a Cash Machine, and that usually means a heavier emphasis on, and an escalation of, marketing and distribution. You can have the best product in the world, but if it's not on the shelf, no one is ever going to see it.

In my eyes, the dune buggy business was going to be this family's fastest path to cash. With their skill sets, this was a business opportunity the entire family could pursue. Mike and the boys could

ONE-YEAR FREEDOM DAY GOALS	
REVENUE	**ASSETS**
FINANCIAL BASELINE	
PRETAX INCOME: *$6,250/month*	**ASSETS:** *$399,500*
EXPENDITURES: *$3,200/month*	**LIABILITIES:** *$211,000*

(**SKILL SET: ADMINISTRATION, ORGANIZATION, BUILDING AND FIXING MECHANICAL ITEMS**)

design and build the vehicles; Mary and the boys could market and sell them. I could see that we could replace Mike's income of $50,000 by making and selling just three of these a year. Carey and Colin were excited about the idea of starting a business with their parents. They'd always enjoyed helping their father make the dune buggies, and they were energized by the thought of working with their mother to market them.

Question 8: Are You Willing to Create and Execute the Wealth Cycle Process?

Both boys were happy to learn they were going to leapfrog their previous aspiration to "go from a blue-collar job to a white-collar job" and skip straight to a "no-collar job."

"It's not enough to think this is a good idea," I said. "We have to create action so that you can prove to yourself, through doing, that you can, in fact, be wealthy. You can't just want it—you must commit to it." Ninety percent of the people I meet are in financial disarray. The fastest way to get clear on what you want and to get your financials organized is to execute. I've found that most of my clients need to act, even if they don't think they're ready. You'll never organize your financials as fast as when you have a mortgage meeting set up at the bank. But if you wait to get organized before you set up the meeting, the wait can become too long. That's why a team approach to making money, with support and knowledge from those who've done it before, is imperative to moving forward fast. You can avoid making mistakes when working with those who know the process.

The couple looked at each other, then at their eager-eyed sons.

"Are you willing to create and execute the Wealth Cycle Process?" I asked. "Say, 'Yes.' "

"Yes," Mike said.

"Yes," Mary said.

"Congratulations," I said. "Yes is the right answer."

Getting down to brass tacks . . .

3

SEQUENCING
The Right Thing at
the Right Time

The television producer asked me to come back and film the second segment where we would map out the plan for the Leonard family to enjoy wealth for the rest of their lives. But she was concerned about Mary not getting a new job.

"This family will have more income than they had when she was working," I said. "And not only that, we'll eliminate their debt, have the college tuition ready to go, and get Mike out of his job."

"Loral, I'm sorry. I hope I told you that we're only filming for six months."

"You did," I said. "We'll have everything up and ready to go so it will be very clear how this will all come to fruition within the next year."

Ready, Hire the Set—Just Go

Once we had an understanding of the Leonard family's current situation and their financial objectives, we began devising ways to increase their earnings. The objective was to create as many income opportunities as possible, through both passive earnings and active businesses. With the information from the eight questions, I suggested a strategy that would not only replace Mary's old salary, and eventually Mike's, but get the family on the road to abundance and prosperity. The Leonard family Gap Analysis is shown below.

ONE-YEAR FREEDOM DAY GOALS	
• *No new job for Mary*	
• *Passive income to replace Mary's salary*	
• *College tuition plan*	
• *Debt elimination plan*	
• *Owning and running their own profitable business*	
REVENUE	*ASSETS*
FINANCIAL BASELINE	
PRETAX INCOME: $6,250/month	*ASSETS: $399,500*
EXPENDITURES: $3,200/month	*LIABILITIES: $211,000*
SKILL SET: Administration, organization, building and fixing mechanical items	

The next step in the Wealth Plan was to create the Wealth Cycle. To do this, we need to put the right building blocks in the right order. As I've noted earlier, the order of the building blocks differs depending on the person and his or her individual needs and objectives. You'll soon be able to see the sequence that's right for you, as noted in the highlighted sequence below, for example.

With the Leonard family, I saw their sequence as follows:

Gap Analysis ➤ Financial Baseline ➤ Freedom Day

Assets ➤ Cash Machine ➤ Entities ➤ Forecasting ➤
Debt Management ➤ Wealth Account

Teamwork + Conditioning + Leadership

As we walk through the Leonard family's sequence, we will take a deeper look at the building blocks, and we will also cover each one in more detail in subsequent chapters.

The Leonard Family's Wealth Plan

The first building block for the Leonard family, and for everyone in the Wealth Cycle Process, is the *Gap Analysis*. The Gap Analysis uncovers the financial gap between where you are now and where you want to be—between your current financial situation and your long-range objectives. This may be a small gap for some of you, but for most of us with a big healthy vision, it's usually a large gap. And believe me when I tell you, this is good news. This gap is not a threat to your ambition; it is, in fact, a necessary element to fueling that very ambition. It should be a motivator.

With the Gap Analysis we cut right to the chase. We don't ask you how you grew up, or what you think about money, or if you truly believe you can be wealthy. We prompt you to take immediate massive action in order to change your situation and move forward. You will believe it when you see it.

For the Leonard family the second building block, the *Financial Baseline,* meant a disappearing salary, credit card debt, and not enough money for the boys to go to college. When you uncover your Financial Baseline, you will understand much more than how much money you have in the bank. You will build your own financial statements, and begin to understand your revenue and expenditures, your assets and liabilities, and know exactly where you are financially. Specifically, you will understand how much money it takes, and what you must do, day-to-day, for you to live the type of life you want.

The third building block for the Leonard family was *Freedom Day.* The one-year goal of this building block was to create enough passive income to replace Mary's salary, get the business going, get rid of debt, and have the college tuition plan in place. A good goal has enough tension to keep you interested and motivated, but it can't be too daunting or you'll get stuck. And getting stuck is not allowed in the Wealth Cycle Process. For years the model of living and dying has been job building, family building, home building, and finally retirement building. Retirement literally means "to retreat from" or "go to sleep" and that just can't be a good goal. Although "retirement" is attached in our society to the age of 65, we want you to enjoy financial freedom at any age. In the Wealth Cycle Process you will forego the idea of retirement and instead envision a Financial Freedom Day.

Now the foundational building blocks for the Leonard family were in place.

Gap Analysis ➤ Financial Baseline ➤ Freedom Day

The next step was to activate the Wealth Cycle. We started with *Assets.* I wanted to assure Mary that she could afford not to go back to work so she could start building their business. The key would be to take current nonperforming assets and get their money working for them. Traditional financial planning ensures that you'll continue to derive 80 percent of your earning capacity after you stop working. I find that very unsatisfying. I have no desire to limit my income and be poorer as I get older. I want to be able to create wealth at any age, and progressively create more as I get older. The Wealth Cycle requires wealth acceleration that goes beyond traditional investment options, such as stocks, bonds, and mutual funds. It requires direct asset allocation into a broader spectrum of opportunities that includes all types of investing in all kinds of industries to build an active and continuous escalation of cash flow and appreciation. Of course, this goes hand-in-hand with building a team of knowledgeable professionals and field partners. No one can get into direct asset allocation without knowledge of those assets—it's too risky. But an experienced wealth-building team, such as the kind we are building in our Team-Made Millionaire community, can give the little guy the same information, leverage, and risk reduction that the big guys have always enjoyed.

Park and Pray and Plan for Poverty

Traditionally, financial advisors have been treated as experts who take care of your money for you, and many of us seem content to let these experts call the shots. I call this the park-and-pray method and I can think of nothing riskier. In this day and age, taking your hard-earned money, parking it with a financial institution, and praying that it increases is, frankly, pathetic. I believe any plan that requires you to cross your fingers is not a good plan. That's like dropping your kids off with someone when they're infants, taking them back when they're 18, and hoping they turned out all right.

The potential for direct investing and asset allocation is infinite. Once you've firmly established your money rules—which are the investing criteria based on both your vision and your values—and your financial goals, then you know the investments that will be right for you. You could become involved in almost any product that offers a return on investment (ROI) that fits your strategy. I usually recommend that one's asset allocation include capital-intensive assets, such as real estate, because these provide the tax benefits of business depreciation with the bonus of cash flow and possible appreciation. My personal investments have always included a lot of real estate, oil and gas, and other capital-intensive businesses.

This type of investing demands the accumulation of a lot of knowledge. This means engaging mentors who've done it all before, because reinventing the wheel is just ridiculous. It means finding field partners who can connect you with the right people in the right assets, because getting inside the community of investors rather than peering over the wall is a much more realistic course of success. And it means putting together a team of experts who will pull you up the learning curve fast, because the Wealth Cycle Process is about action, not theory. The Wealth Cycle Process demands direct investment in a diverse number of assets. The difference between direct and indirect investing is the difference between driving a car and holding onto the back bumper for dear life.

In order to activate the Wealth Cycle Process, the Leonard family needed to make direct investments that met their goals. There are generally two types of investments: income investments that create cash flow and growth investments that build equity. Because Mary had lost her job, the Leonard family needed cash flow. In order to replace Mary's income, we needed to shift some of the Leonard family's assets, such as the equity in their home and their mutual funds, into these cash flow–producing assets. As we saw earlier, Mike and Mary had $399,500 of assets:

- $350,000 in equity in their house
- $30,000 in IRAs
- $16,000 in mutual funds for the boys
- $1,500 in cash, savings account
- $2,000 in stocks

and they were willing to

1. Take $100,000 of the equity out of their house through a re-financing.
2. Shift the $30,000 from their IRAs into a self-directed IRA that would allow them to choose the investments. (While there are many self-directed IRAs at large brokerage firms, there are only a handful of *true* self-directed IRA companies that will support the type of asset allocation we're doing here. To find one of these, you can email me at IRA@liveoutloud.com.)
3. Move the $16,000 in the boys' mutual funds to a better income-producing asset for their college tuition.
4. Use the $2,000 in stocks from Mary's grandmother for something else.

These measures allowed a total of $148,000 to be directly allocated into a diverse range of unconventional income-generating assets. My wealth team and I helped Mike and Mary consider several choices. The Leonard family wealth-building measures are shown below.

Leonard Family Choices for Wealth Building

ONE-YEAR FREEDOM DAY GOALS
- *No new job for Mary*
- *Passive income to replace Mary's salary*
- *College tuition plan*
- *Debt elimination plan*
- *Owning and running their own profitable business*

REVENUE	ASSETS
CASH MACHINE	SHIFT $148,000 OF ASSETS
PASSIVE INCOME	

CASH FLOW:

$2,000/month cash flow from real estate properties

$300/month cash flow from real estate properties

$320/month from note

APPRECIATION:

Year 1: $52,000

Year 2: $67,600

- *$60,000 to real estate, for 10 cash flow–producing rental properties. ($200/month)*
- *$16,000 to real estate for 2 cash flow–producing rental properties ($150/month)*
- *$32,000 in promissory note at 12%*
- *$40,000 to real estate, for appreciating properties*

FINANCIAL BASELINE

PRETAX INCOME: $6,250/month   *ASSETS: $399,500*

EXPENDITURES: $3,200/month   *LIABILITIES: $211,000*

SKILL SET: Administration, organization, building and fixing mechanical items

By simply reallocating a little more than half of the family's assets, Mary's one-year Freedom Day goal of not having to go to work was already in motion. We'd more than replaced Mary's monthly income of $2,080 a month with passive income of $2,620 a month. Additionally, by buying assets with depreciation and expenses that once the family's business entities were structured, could be written off as expenditures against the revenue, Mike and Mary would retain much more of their earnings. And that was just shifting assets. We hadn't even begun to create the Cash Machine.

Turning Assets into Other Assets

1. **Equity into cash.** The question that may be in your head right now is how to turn equity—in this example we're talking about home equity—into the cash to actually make these direct asset allocations—in this example, real estate investments. There are several ways to take equity out of your home to create cash: for example, through a home equity loan or by refinancing at the higher valuation. There are pluses and minuses to both approaches; the former would increase your liabilities and the latter would increase your mortgage payment. My wealth-building team includes several good mortgage brokers and direct asset allocation specialists who know how to think creatively about these transactions. You should include these professionals on your team.

Converting equity to cash is not difficult, and the benefits of pumping up an underperforming asset far outweigh any extra paperwork. If you choose a solid, performing asset to invest the cash in, you don't increase your risk. Many of us have been conditioned to believe that a home is the nest egg of all nest eggs and the equity in it is too fragile to touch. The only way to wealth, though, is to invest in assets that generate healthy returns. Your home equity can help you do that, and if you conduct careful research and get the help of experts, you're doing with your own money exactly what the bank would be doing with it if they had it. There's no one better than you to make money from your money.

2. Cash flow–producing assets. Real estate that creates monthly cash flow is usually inexpensive real estate with little appreciation and a steady stream of reliable renters. In the Leonards' case, we paid $6,000 in cash for each of the 10 homes. This $6,000 bought a home valued at $45,000, with a 10 percent down payment, $4,500, plus $1,500 for closing costs. The rent on the property was $695. The principal, interest, taxes, and insurance (PITI) plus the equity line payment for the refinancing, and management fees equaled $495. The remainder was the $200 monthly cash flow. These numbers will vary depending on the investor's credit rating and other factors. In the case of the second property, you may wonder why we didn't just put all the money into that first asset, which cost less and is producing more. But in direct asset allocation, you may not always have access to all the properties you desire, and you may want to diversify with other field partners.

3. Promissory notes. Within our community of wealth builders, businesses constantly lend other businesses money. This provides a convenient source of funds for the borrower and a nice healthy return for the lender. Obviously, the borrower must agree to full disclosure and the lender must embark on due diligence to ensure a successful transaction, and both parties must have experienced legal and tax advice regarding the transaction.

4. Appreciating assets. It's important to note that the type of real estate appreciation we're seeing in our community requires direct investment in bread-and-butter regions. Investing in super-appreciating markets such as Florida, Nevada, and Arizona in 2005, for example, would have put you in a situation where rising interest rates could slow those markets down. Not only can this get you turned upside down, paying out more cash than you're taking in each month, but it can send housing prices down rather than up. If you're smart about your strategy and the markets you choose, you plan for market fluctuations.

Teamwork: Less Risk, More Reward

This is the type of hands-on, nontraditional, direct investing the Wealth Cycle requires. Although many financial advisors may scream that there is risk involved in taking money out of one's home, and most people are using their equity to pay down debt, why not use it for growth assets? I believe it is much less risky to actively manage your investments than to park and pray. There's no market swinging up and down at the whim of a few Dow Jones industrials, no mismanagement of assets, and no hodgepodge bundle of good and bad assets under one umbrella. It's your money, your field partner, your team, your revenue, and your say. I can't stress enough the importance of teamwork and due diligence—that is, the practice of researching and investigating every investment—in this approach. The investor must be fully engaged; the Wealth Cycle Process does not allow for passivity. And because most of us don't have all the time in the world to build our wealth, especially when we have to work a full-time job in the meantime, the team approach is the only approach to money making that really works. By working side-by-side with experienced millionaires, you put yourself in a position to create wealth faster than you ever thought possible.

Back to the Leonards. In a few minutes, we'd given the family a strategy that didn't include replacing Mary's job, but did generate almost $32,000 of passive income a year. Mike and Mary Leonard couldn't believe it. While passive income from the direct asset allocation was great and the Leonard family could certainly have lived on this, this shifting of assets would only sustain them at, or slightly above, their current income level. This was not enough. A wealth builder needs to build wealth, and that means accelerating the Wealth Cycle by making more money by establishing a *Cash Machine.* To begin with, this would mean creating a business and getting one's hands dirty. But very soon, it would mean running the business and hiring others to do the work. For example, a teacher may start a tutoring business, even if that's the last thing she wants to do, just to learn entrepreneurship and generate immediate revenue. But then she'll hire others to do the tutoring, probably colleagues, and focus on marketing and managing the business.

Wealth builders become entrepreneurs who know how to run a business. In the Wealth Cycle Process, you must learn to earn more money from a business venture. Not only will the business revenue supplement the passive income from the assets, but the business entity will provide a vehicle for maximizing tax strategies. The business is the Cash Machine in that it creates money to fuel the Wealth Cycle.

You've Got Skill$

Entrepreneurship is the single biggest source of wealth in this country, and by establishing your own business you can increase and keep more of your cash. I coached the Leonard family to establish their Cash Machine. It can take a business venture several months to get up and running, but the marketing initiative has to start immediately. I always try to get my coaching clients to shoot for a 120-

day goal of finding buyers and generating cash. It seemed to me that the Leonards' Cash Machine was dune buggies.

"I'm not sure I want to run my own business," Mike said. "That's too risky."

"And I just want to get a job again, something like my old job," Mary said.

"No, you don't," I said. "You are putting your financial future at too great a risk by working for other people and letting money managers handle your investments. You have the ability to be millionaires, so why not do it?"

Mike shrugged. "I guess we're scared."

"Well," I said. "At least that's a reason I can understand."

They are not alone in being scared. Though I have made more money than I ever thought possible, I've also made many mistakes along the way. I've made bad investments and bad choices, and I've lost money. Most wealthy people have. It's part of the learning curve. But ultimately I made good investments and good choices, and I never made the same mistake twice. By giving myself permission to fail as part of my overall learning experience, I began to live outside of my comfort zone. As a result, that comfort zone expands daily. One of my mentors once told me that when my annual income becomes my monthly income, I'd just be getting started with wealth building. That seemed unbelievable to me. Now there are times when I make that kind of money in a single day.

Action has created the experience that gave me the evidence to know that I am on the right track. And because I've built a great team of trusted professionals and colleagues—as you will do—I'm constantly supported and able to weave around the landmines as I grow. In the Wealth Cycle Process we focus on businesses that can contribute to the Wealth Cycle immediately. As exciting as it may seem to run your own ice-cream company, open a hotel, invent a new running shoe, or even establish a charitable organization, those ideas are long-term goals toward which your Wealth Cycle Process will propel you—not the short-term strategies that help you learn to earn.

In order to learn to earn and keep what they earn, I require my clients to create an entity, that is, a corporation or partnership or limited liability company (LLC) that supports a viable business strategy based on their existing skill set, so that they can make real money and gain experience running a business. Then they can achieve bigger and more exciting entrepreneurial visions. Again, it's important not to let the need to create an entity scare you away from this process. It's easy. And the resources in this book give you all the information you will need to get started. Billionaires don't go home at night and pay the bills out of their personal checking account. Those tycoons are where they are today because they mastered the skill of creating companies to support their visions.

My wealth team and I sat down with the Leonard family and built a business directive, a scaled-down version of a business plan, to develop and market the business. (Creating a business directive is covered in more detail in Chapter 5.) It seemed to me that the Leonards' number one task in refocusing this hobby into a viable business would be marketing and distribution—finding customers. In order to stem start-up costs, the Leonards would have to presell their first dune buggy. In addition, our team thought that by customizing the product, the family could consider an initial price point of $20,000 per dune buggy. As they learned how to market and sell their product, they could forecast to sell more sophisticated models at $100,000 each.

Potentially, the Cash Machine could generate more than $5,000 in revenue a month, allowing Mike to leave behind the $4,000 a month he was getting from his job. Eventually, as their volume and prices increased, the Leonard family could reach their now seemingly too small goal of $6,250 a month of cash flow, just from the Cash Machine. It's interesting to note the risk Mike would really be taking in starting this business. With his skill set, he would always be able to find a salaried job as a mechanic. That's his real safety net. But safety nets aren't the road to wealth. Though Mike may have a little to lose in his pursuit of a Cash Machine in terms of time, energy, and money, he has a huge amount to gain. For instance, the entity established for this business would provide a structure to protect a lot of the family's revenue.

Next, the Leonard family needed to structure *Entities* for the management of their direct investments (for example, real estate) and for the manufacturing and marketing of the dune buggies. For example,

1. Trusts
2. C corporations, S corporations, and limited liability companies (LLC)
3. Limited partnerships

Under the U.S. Tax Code, assets held in these entities are treated differently than an individual's personal assets. These entities often retain more cash than an individual possibly could; this helps the entity, and its assets, to create more cash flow. Most people were encouraged and trained to become sole proprietors and salaried workers—that is, good employees. Few of the wealthy are good employees. Every single wealthy person I know has done it inside a corporate structure, taking full advantage of the highest tax savings allowed by law. Having a job or being a professional need not be mutually exclusive from creating an optimal tax entity for your wealth generation activities. Entity structuring is imperative in the Wealth Cycle Process in order to take full advantage of the Tax

Code and hold onto more of your hard-earned money. Entities are the difference between having your money going into your Social Security account or into your company's employer identification number for federal tax identification.

In the Wealth Cycle Process, you need to get your house in order. By setting up your life as a business you start thinking like a business, and that means becoming a profitable and productive entity. With entity structuring, you will establish companies, partnerships, and trusts that will give your money a place to flow into and out of. This will help you better manage your millions and keep you focused on your asset allocation and passive income. For the Leonard family, we recommended they set up several entities:

1. An LLC for their real estate properties
2. An LLC for the boys' real estate properties
3. An S corporation to market the dune buggies
4. A trust to serve as an umbrella for all of their companies and holdings

As the Leonard family increases their business and their profitability we'll also consider bringing in a C corporation to manage the other businesses, a strategy we'll explain in Chapter 6. The initial cost for setting up each of these entities, usually around $600 with the help of a knowledgeable professional, will be more than covered by the revenue they retain each year.

The next building block *Forecasting*, sets up your tax strategy by building a chart of accounts. For every wealth builder this means a full accounting of revenue generation from business and investing activities as well as a projection of spending to support these activities.

The chart of accounts for the Leonard family looked like this:

	PERSONAL	LLC (REAL ESTATE)	LLC (BOYS' REAL ESTATE)	S CORP. (MARKET DUNE BUGGIES)	C CORP. (MANAGE OTHER BUSINESSES)	TOTAL
REVENUE						
EXPENDITURES						
ASSETS						
LIABILITIES						

While the family would have to hire a bookkeeper and therefore code their expenses, they should not be caught up in doing this paperwork. It is not a good use of any wealth builder's time. This chart is what will establish the fine line between what you keep and what you give to the government.

For the next building block, *Debt Management,* the Leonard family would follow the Five-Step Debt Elimination Plan, as described in Chapter 9 so that they could rid themselves of their credit card debt. This step, which would begin immediately, shows how each phase of the wealth-building process is carried out almost concurrently. The sequence of the Leonard family's building blocks is as follows:

Assets → Cash Machine → Entities → Forecasting → Debt Management → Wealth Account

Yet debt management begins almost the day that asset allocation is set in motion, and the Wealth Account Priority Payment (WAPP) is made at the same time that the debt payments are made.

Bad Debt Is the Greatest Barrier to Wealth

Eliminating bad debt is an essential building block of the Wealth Cycle. If you're paying high interest on credit card debt, you are losing precious dollars that could be used to invest and make much more money. The compounding interest of money is exponential, as those of you in debt know all too well. But interest also compounds up, so spending money before you've earned it, or spending money before you've invested it, is like stealing from yourself. Bad debt has got to go. The Wealth Cycle Process's Five-Step Debt Elimination Plan removes debt and creates wealth simultaneously, so you do not have to wait for one to get to the other.

The next step in the sequence for the Leonard family was to set up a *Wealth Account*, as well as a WAPP, to ensure that a portion of the earnings from Mike's salary, as well as the income from the new business and investments, would be set aside for investments. This is essential in order to keep fueling the assets. As we structure this family's wealth plan, we'll set up their personal and corporate Wealth Accounts and priority payment systems.

A Dollar Saved Is a Dollar of Delayed Spending

By spending what we earn most of us are skipping over this fundamental action necessary to generate wealth—namely, creating the Wealth Account. The Wealth Account is a specific interest-bearing account in a brokerage firm from which you can draw to invest in even more rewarding opportunities, such as real estate and business ventures. Even if the money is only in an interest-bearing cash account, and there are now institutions that give as much as 3 percent interest, you'll soon be able to accumulate enough money to start investing. Once the Wealth Account is established you will start the practice of paying yourself first. Every month you will deposit a fixed amount into your Wealth Account, preferably an amount automatically withdrawn from your paycheck or corporate account.

As the money in the Wealth Account grows, it is put to work in assets that generate cash flow. In the Wealth Cycle Process you will invest in assets that produce passive income and reinvest that passive income into new assets to produce more consistent passive income. This cycle of turning income into assets, and assets into income, is the key to building sustainable wealth. The money works for you, not you for it, and you focus your attention on maximizing your rates of return.

There's No Such Thing as a Self-Made Millionaire

The Wealth Cycle Process must include three other essential building blocks: Teamwork, Leadership, and Conditioning. The Wealth Cycle Process is contingent upon the concept of *Teamwork*, that is, Team-Made Millionaires. People who tell you they built wealth without a team to help them are not telling the whole truth. In order to redirect their assets, start their business, and structure entities and forecast, the Leonard family was going to need a good team.

Professional advisors, colleagues, and field partners with opportunities, not to mention lawyers, accountants, and supportive partners, are crucial to creating wealth. In the Wealth Cycle Process it is your job to direct a team of professionals that helps you to develop and execute your strategy for building wealth. You cannot and should not try to be an expert in all the fields asset generation requires. You just need to find the experts, get them on your team, and lead them to your goal. The lone rangers ramming their way to wealth are a myth. No one does it alone. Even those who stand alone, whether a national tennis champion or the CEO of the largest software company in the world or the president of the United States, have a team providing guidance, assistance, and support. Wealthy people realize that experienced and skilled professionals are worth their weight in gold. Not only does this minimize the tedium, but it gives the money the best chance to succeed.

And it's not just the skilled professionals who are necessary to make a team flourish. It also means bringing in the utility players. In my view, if you are a wealth builder, you should never clean your house again. Those are tasks you can pay someone else to do and you can spend those hours creating wealth. I call it the $400 Solution. If you hired out work, such as housecleaning, gardening, or shopping, at $10 an hour, then just an extra $100 a week would free up 10 more hours for you. In a month that's $400 to give you 40 more hours to focus on your wealth. That's a whole workweek you just got back to build wealth. In my work with clients, the number one excuse I hear is, "I don't have enough time." The $400 Solution makes that excuse go away. And if $400 seems like too much, try $200, or $100 a month. Those hourly fees will more than repay themselves. I always say, "If you don't have time, you need a team."

Wealthy people also create a circle of trusted field partners and advisors with whom they discuss deals and create opportunities. Contrary to popular opinion, you don't want to be the smartest person in the room. You want to be with people who have bigger, better brains, not to mention more experience. That's what creates Team-Made Millionaires. If you are spending your time with people who have the same net worth as you do and who make you feel comfortable, you are not going to stretch and grow. You want to be constantly learning with a team, which is the most efficient and effective road to wealth.

Because the Wealth Cycle Process is contingent upon direct investing, a good team is vital. In order to locate the optimal direct investments, you need a cadre of field partners. These are people who are in the field, who know the industry, the region, and the players in the arena you want to invest in. They provide the connections, legwork, and oversight, while you provide the cash, the credit, or the network of investors. Field partners include such people as realtors, chamber of commerce members, business brokers, and regional financial planners.

Finding the best people for your wealth team is crucial to your success, and once you've voiced your vision and taken action to move toward it, others will be compelled by your leadership to join your pursuit. And you'll join others in their pursuit, because you'll also discover that helping others helps you. That's what we do in our Team-Made Millionaire community. For those who swirl in the highest socioeconomic circles, sharing opportunities has always been part of the status quo. For centuries, the wealthy have understood that since it takes money to make money, and more money makes more money, it's smart to spread the word— and the wealth. All who are on the way to greater wealth should find, cultivate, and network with like-minded people.

Obviously, the Leonard family had a lot of *Conditioning* to do. They saw themselves as a blue-collar family working until the day they die. They needed to see themselves as wealth builders with a million-dollar business. Most approaches start with psychology, with changing your mindset and making it the genesis for changing your behavior. Now, while I'm a big fan of psychology, I've also studied enough human behavior to see that this approach gives you permission to fail, and I don't want you to fail. I only succeed if you succeed, and I won't ask you to try to think your way to success. This building block is about where you've been and your relationship to money, that is, your conditioning.

As we move forward with your Wealth Cycle Process we will create a new conversation around money that restates past beliefs culled from where you've been, and clarifies your vision of where you're going. Together, we will take a step-by-step, action-oriented approach that will change your behavior, then change your thinking and make you wealthy. But it will not be done in your head. It will be done through your hands, and you will make this happen. You will, in fact, run into your psychology as you create a positive cycle of wealth acceleration. Your financial conditioning, the psychology and relationship you have with money, is something that you must begin to be aware of, to manage and steer the rest of your life. Mike and Mary Leonard took the first big step in confronting their conditioning by agreeing to be coached by me, take a new approach to wealth, and have a new conversation about money.

When my clients want to be coached by me, the first requirement is that they are willing to do it my way. While their way has been interesting, it hasn't been helpful; otherwise, they would already have reached their goals. In following the Wealth Cycle Process, you'll notice that you have to first surrender and then relearn what you know, and this will be a little uncomfortable. But then you will own it.

Wealthy people take a *Leadership* role in their wealth plan: they literally lead their wealth. Though you may, and should, choose to delegate the activities that support your wealth building, no one can drive it like you can. If you do not keep consistent and constant pressure on the gas, the wealth engine will sputter to a stop. No one cares as much as you do about your wealth and your leadership is crucial to your success. You, and only you, will assume the leadership role to learn about and execute the building blocks in the Wealth Cycle. Inertia is easy in the short term but painful over time. It's your decision to remain where you are, but if you dig in your heels and take charge of your life, you will arrive at a better place.

The Bigger, Better Game

After the second segment was shot, the television producer called. "I can't believe what you did, Loral," she said. "You took a blue-collar family that was dealing with a job loss and totally replaced the mom's salary by—what did you call it? Oh yeah, waking up their lazy assets. And their kids are now walking around with business cards that say Daredevil Dune Buggies Company and explaining these sophisticated business entities and tax strategies to me that I thought were only for guys like my boss. You've got them climbing up out of debt, and they're actually building wealth. Real wealth."

"That's a happy day," I said.

"Think you could do this trick again?"

"It's not a trick, and yes. I can do it again and again and again."

Money makes money go round . . .

4

DIRECT ASSET ALLOCATION
Assets to Income,
Income to Assets

The secret to building wealth is investing in assets that create more assets, and Assets are an integral building block of the Wealth Cycle.

Albert Einstein said, "The eighth wonder of the world is the compounding power of money." Investing is a lifelong process that you should begin as early as possible and manage throughout your life. It's the process of continually building your asset pool. As you become more sophisticated, you will reallocate those assets to get higher and higher returns. If you are starting late in this process, there is no need to be discouraged: this approach will work for you wherever you are in life. I believe you can become a millionaire in three to five years after establishing your Financial Baseline and freeing yourself of consumer debt. Most successful investors got that way by investing small amounts of money consistently, year after year, until they accumulated increasingly larger amounts. They continually reinvested their profits and added additional money to their accounts when possible. The majority added to their investment choices monthly and consistently reallocated their funds to diversify their assets.

Patterns of Money

There's never been a better time to create wealth. This information age in which we live has spawned global opportunities never before available and the technology to collect the information to access these opportunities. It's time to understand how to create a Wealth Cycle.

In order to activate and sustain the Wealth Cycle mechanism, you must

1. Earmark a portion of your earnings to put into a Wealth Account every month. This is your Wealth Account Priority Payment (WAPP), which we detail later in Chapter 8.
2. Invest the money in the Wealth Account directly into carefully investigated and researched cash-creating and cash-appreciating investment opportunities, that is, assets that produce passive income and/or equity.
3. Reinvest the passive income you make to create more assets and produce more passive income.
4. Set up Entities to protect these assets and the passive income they generate.
5. Maximize tax strategies, given the entities you've established, by Forecasting the right spending into the right accounts.
6. Create a Cash Machine—an entrepreneurial venture—to accelerate the Wealth Cycle. Earmark a portion of your company's revenue to go into a special Holding Account that will act like a personal Wealth Account and will be used to

invest in assets. Soon, this holding account will essentially become your own bank, lending money to your other companies for investments.

This cycle of turning income into assets and assets into income is the process of building sustainable wealth. The money works for you, not you for it, and you focus your energies and attention on maximizing your rates of return. Rick Noonan, a member of our Team-Made Millionaire and Big Table communities, was a classic example of someone who didn't understand effective asset allocation.

Busy but Not Productive

Rick and his wife live outside Seattle with their three kids. When I met Rick, he had a whole lot of assets and absolutely no clue. He was worried. Though their finances seemed under control, at age 36, he felt that he and his wife were constantly "busy, but not productive," that he'd become indentured to his job at a consumer products company, and that he'd created a lifestyle he wasn't sure he could sustain into retirement. Driving two hours to and from work every day for a 10-hour-a-day job that was neither here nor there for him, he seemed to me a man committed to the commute. I see that a lot. People are so busy racing to do what they're trapped into doing that they don't step back to realize that the running and racing about isn't working. Few of us rarely take the time to reevaluate our lives. I asked Rick what better use could he make of those 20 hours a week of driving time and how much improved his life might be if he weren't pushing through five days to live for a weekend crammed with activities.

Many people sitting on more debt and a low five-figure salary might look at Rick's situation and wonder what he has to complain about. But as most of us know, whether you're spiraling in debt or consistently uncertain about your capacity to cover your monthly nut, finances can create a good deal of stress and worry. The better situation would be to have wealth and abundance and financial freedom, and the capacity to focus your attention and energies on family and friends, health and adventure, spirituality and other life-affirming experiences. The nice thing about the wealth-building process is that when people reach their Freedom Day, having changed their behavior and subsequently their way of being, they become whole new people.

We drew out the schematic for his Gap Analysis, and Rick answered the eight questions in just under eight minutes with no problem.

Question 1:What Is Your Monthly Income?

"My wife makes $70,000 a year, I make $80,000 a year, but that's before taxes."

ONE-YEAR FREEDOM DAY GOALS	
REVENUE	ASSETS
FINANCIAL BASELINE	
PRETAX INCOME: $12,500/month	ASSETS:
EXPENDITURES:	LIABILITIES:
SKILL SET:	

- $5,800 Rick's wife's salary
- $6,700 Rick's salary
- No entities, no business, personal bank account

Question 2: What Are Your Monthly Expenditures?

"After taxes, we barely break even. We spend about $7,000 a month," Rick said. Then he shrugged. "Though I don't really know. We should really get one of those software programs, shouldn't we?"

ONE-YEAR FREEDOM DAY GOALS	
REVENUE	ASSETS
FINANCIAL BASELINE	
PRETAX INCOME: $12,500/month	ASSETS:
(EXPENDITURES: $7,000/month)	LIABILITIES:
SKILL SET:	
• Manual bookkeeping	

Question 3: What Assets Do You Have?

"A lot, actually," Rick said. "I know we have about $300,000 of equity in our house, and I'm positive I have about $50,000 in my current company's stock. But I can't get that out."

Unless he left the company, which I knew I'd be convincing him to do sooner rather than later. I'm always amazed when couples invest in real estate while both work as salaried employees for companies. Under IRS rules, real estate depreciation is limited to $25,000 a year unless a person is a professional real estate investor. The Noonans were likely giving up thousands in deductible dollars, just to keep their jobs.

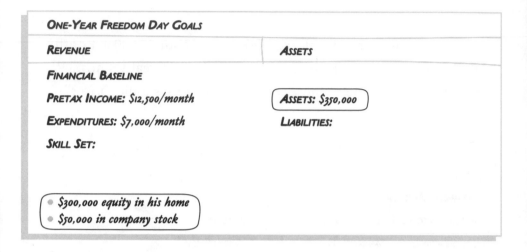

ONE-YEAR FREEDOM DAY GOALS

REVENUE	ASSETS
FINANCIAL BASELINE	
PRETAX INCOME: $12,500/month	ASSETS: $350,000
EXPENDITURES: $7,000/month	LIABILITIES:
SKILL SET:	

- $300,000 equity in his home
- $50,000 in company stock

Question 4: What Are Your Liabilities?

"We still have an $85,000 mortgage on the house, but we're paying that down."

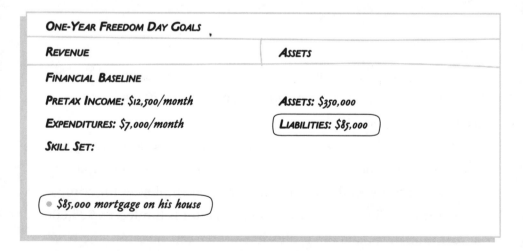

ONE-YEAR FREEDOM DAY GOALS

REVENUE	ASSETS
FINANCIAL BASELINE	
PRETAX INCOME: $12,500/month	ASSETS: $350,000
EXPENDITURES: $7,000/month	LIABILITIES: $85,000
SKILL SET:	

- $85,000 mortgage on his house

Question 5: What Else?

"We have $10,000 in the bank. And I have $40,000 in an IRA and my wife has $30,000 in her IRA," Rick said. "And I actually have a few 401(k)s from past jobs. Between my wife and me, there are four of them: we have $60,000 there."

ONE-YEAR FREEDOM DAY GOALS

REVENUE	ASSETS
FINANCIAL BASELINE	
PRETAX INCOME: $12,500/month	**ASSETS: $490,000**
EXPENDITURES: $7,000/month	**LIABILITIES:** $85,000
SKILL SET:	

- $70,000 in IRAs
- $60,000 in old company 401(k)s
- $10,000 in cash

Question 6: What Do You Want?

As with everyone, this took Rick a few minutes to conjure up. I've noticed that it takes a lot of prompting to get people to dream these days. They usually answer this with a safe and doable goal, because they're feeling trapped and frustrated, so they stop dreaming. Most people have a vision of only what they don't want, and position themselves away from, not toward, their dreams. It's time to dig around in your attic of lost dreams and reconnect with them, because if you want to be in a bigger, better game, you have to think bigger and better. Given a realistic, reasonable, but insistent time frame and specific accountabilities, I believe these dreams can come true.

"My wife and I would like to take care of the college tuition for our kids and pursue a fun life, with no jobs," he said. I asked him to quantify this. "I would like two million bucks to invest and five thousand dollars a month in passive income."

"Five thousand a month?" I said.

"Yeah," Rick said. "Is that too much?"

This is very common. People just have no ideas what the reality is for viable returns. If Rick wanted $5,000 a month on $2 million, he was looking for a pathetic annual return. Egads, shoot me.

"Rick, in my community of wealth builders we're going for 10, 20, 30 percent returns, at least. That's the kind of asset allocation we're doing. Aggressive, unconventional, direct. If we don't get those kind of returns, we don't play. We move on."

"Ah, so you're saying that my number is too low?"

"Right," I said. "But let's get realistic. Let's double your net worth from approximately $400,000 to $800,000 and give you a conservative 12 percent return."

His fingers danced on a calculator. "That's $10,000 a month. Hey that's double what I said I wanted."

"Is that big enough for you?" I said.

He shifted back in his seat. "Are you guaranteeing me that type of return?"

I shook my head fast. "I'm educating you to look for that type of return. I'm your mentor and your coach, and I'm going to show you how millionaires scour for assets that generate wealth. You are not going to play someone else's game, Rick. You're going to lead your own. Instead of giving the market or anyone else all those commissions and fees to make money with your money, you're going to do what they do once they have your money. You're going to go invest in direct and diversified assets and get those higher returns for yourself."

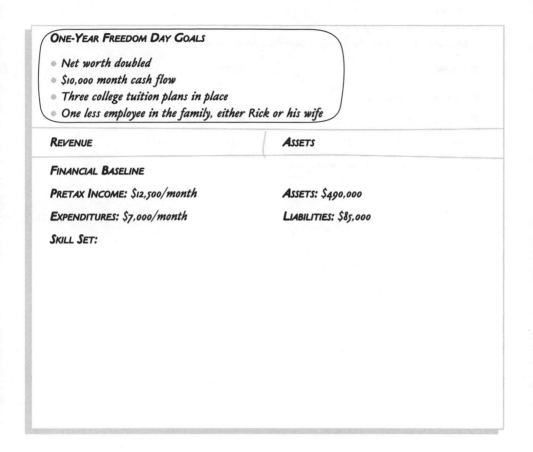

ONE-YEAR FREEDOM DAY GOALS

- *Net worth doubled*
- *$10,000 month cash flow*
- *Three college tuition plans in place*
- *One less employee in the family, either Rick or his wife*

REVENUE	ASSETS
FINANCIAL BASELINE	
PRETAX INCOME: $12,500/month	**ASSETS:** $490,000
EXPENDITURES: $7,000/month	**LIABILITIES:** $85,000
SKILL SET:	

Question 7: What Skills Do You Use to Make Money?

Gap Analysis   Cash Machine

"I'm in marketing, and so is my wife. Consumer brand products."

"But what are those skills?"

"Basic marketing, I guess," Rick said. "Brand management, budgeting, pricing the product, product development and packaging, distribution, promotions, ads, stuff like that."

ONE-YEAR FREEDOM DAY GOALS

- *Net worth doubled*
- *$10,000 month cash flow*
- *Three college tuition plans in place*
- *One less employee in the family, either Rick or his wife*

REVENUE	ASSETS

FINANCIAL BASELINE

PRETAX INCOME: *$12,500/month*   **ASSETS:** *$490,000*

EXPENDITURES: *$7,000/month*   **LIABILITIES:** *$85,000*

(**SKILL SET:** *Marketing, brand management*)

Question 8: Are You Willing to Create and Execute the Wealth Cycle Process?

Gap Analysis   Leadership

"Yes," he said.

"Yes is the right answer," I said.

Eight questions in eight minutes. Rick's Gap Analysis looked like this:

ONE-YEAR FREEDOM DAY GOALS

- *Net worth doubled*
- *$10,000 month cash flow*
- *Three college tuition plans in place*
- *One less employee in the family, either Rick or his wife*

REVENUE

ASSETS

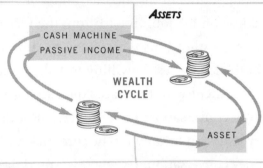

CASH MACHINE
PASSIVE INCOME

WEALTH
CYCLE

ASSET

FINANCIAL BASELINE

PRETAX INCOME: *$12,500/month*　　　　　**ASSETS:** *$490,000*

EXPENDITURES: *$7,000/month*　　　　　　**LIABILITIES:** *$85,000*

SKILL SET: *Marketing, brand management*

- *$300,000 equity in own home*
- *$50,000 in company stock*
- *$70,000 in IRAs*
- *$60,000 in old company 401(k)s*
- *$10,000 in cash*
- *$85,000 mortgage on own home*

Given that Rick had such badly invested assets, and no structure to his wealth, I saw the building blocks of his Wealth Cycle sequence in this way.

Gap Analysis ➤ Financial Baseline ➤ Freedom Day

Assets ➤ Entities ➤ Forecasting ➤ Wealth Account ➤
Cash Machine ➤ Debt Management

Leadership + Conditioning + Teamwork

Rick Noonan's Wealth Plan

As for everyone in the Wealth Cycle Process, the first building block for Rick was the Gap Analysis. In Rick's *Gap Analysis,* we were able to uncover several lazy assets, a lack of entities and tax strategies so that he was retaining little of his income, and a need to focus more on his life and less on his job. In addition, the fact that Rick had come to me alone, without his wife, made me think that she was uninterested in their finances, unwilling to talk about their money with a coach, or content with the status quo, seeing no need to engage in a financial conversation. Fully 76 percent of divorces are because of money issues, so I wanted to be sure Rick and his wife were having the money conversation. I knew this would have to come up in Rick's conditioning, leadership, and teamwork building blocks if he was going to fully engage in, and accelerate, the Wealth Cycle Process.

The *Financial Baseline* revealed that Rick was asset-heavy and those assets were not doing much for him. We needed to increase their capacity, through better asset allocation, entities, forecasting, and the creation of a Cash Machine to invest in more assets. The extent of his expenditures also indicated that he could benefit from better tax strategies and expense management. It was evident that Rick, a man committed to the commute, was going to run headlong into his conditioning, not to mention his wife, on his way to his *Freedom Day.* Given his current situation, he could start replacing his own salary with passive income with just a small shift of his assets. If Rick traded his commitment to his commute for a commitment to his wealth, his wealth could explode. We had to get Rick's money working hard for him, instead of him working hard for his money. His next building block was *Assets.*

The wealthy are not in the market—the wealthy control the market. If Rick wanted to do what the wealthy do, he could no longer park-and-pray his money at 6 percent with a broker. To me, that's like fast-food finance. It's convenient; you drive through, order from a limited menu, and consume predictable mediocrity. Rick had to increase his passive income by fueling and accelerating his Wealth Cycle with a specific plan of direct and diversified asset allocation. Rick had a lot of opportunity to engage the Wealth Cycle through his Assets. Rick's total assets of $490,000 consisted of

- $300,000 equity in his own home
- $50,000 in current company's stock
- $70,000 in IRAs
- $60,000 in old company 401(k)s
- $10,000 in cash

And Rick was willing to

1. Take $140,000 of the equity out of his house, in a refinancing
2. Shift the $70,000 from their IRAs into a true self-directed IRA
3. Move the $60,000 from old 401(k)s for a total of $270,000 in assets that could be directly allocated into a diverse range of unconventional and aggressive income generating assets

My wealth team and I helped him consider several choices.

ONE-YEAR FREEDOM DAY GOALS
- Net worth doubled
- $10,000 month cash flow
- Three college tuition plans in place
- One less employee in the family, either Rick or his wife

REVENUE

PASSIVE INCOME

CASH FLOW:
$2,800/month
$600/month
$3,000/month

APPRECIATION:
Year 1: $56,000
Year 2: $67,000

ASSETS

SHIFT ASSETS OF $270,000:
- $70,000 into a start-up company, 48% return
- $60,000 promissory note at 12%
- $90,000 in 15 bread-and-butter cash flow houses, in two different markets, at $6,000 each, $200/month cash flow
- $50,000 in four preconstruction houses

FINANCIAL BASELINE

PRETAX INCOME: $12,500/month

EXPENDITURES: $7,000/month

SKILL SET: Marketing, brand management

ASSETS: $490,000

LIABILITIES: $85,000

- $300,000 equity in own home
- $50,000 in company stock
- $70,000 in IRAs
- $60,000 in old company 401(k)s
- $10,000 in cash (to be used for Cash Machine start-up costs)
- $85,000 mortgage on his home

This shifting of assets gave Rick $6,400 in cash flow a month, several aggressively appreciating direct assets, and great depreciation to use against his income. Also, because each of these investments would be held within an entity, he would be able to deduct several of his expenses associated with these assets, such as the lease on the car he would use to drive to all the meetings. The day we did the eight-minute exercise with him was a happy one for Mr. Rick

Noonan. And once he got his entities and forecasting in order, Rick was able to have his assets create more assets until he was finally ready to be a W-2 no more. That's when his wealth really took off.

Asset Addicts

Some of these asset allocations may seem daunting and inaccessible to you. But nothing in the finance world is as sophisticated as it appears, and no one in the finance world is smarter or more capable than anyone who has the capacity to read this book. When you collect information by reading the trade newspapers and magazines and start engaging in conversations with people in these fields, you'll see that, if everyone stopped talking so fast, the simplicity of it all would surface.

The tactics we suggest for asset allocation are not mainstream tactics. But we believe that this is one arena where not following the crowd can be the most profitable choice of all. I personally use these techniques, as do many of my peers and clients, even those with little previous finance or investing expertise, let alone available cash. In fact, I can safely say that most of us have joined the Asset Addicts program. Though they may seem aggressive, these investment opportunities are legal, sound, and well within the customary risk-reward scale.

Diversification and Flexibility

Diversifying is the art of investing in many opportunities, rather than just one or two investments. Some people are wary of overextending their interests. Fortunately, growing up in a small town, I was conditioned to do this. If we didn't play sports, act in the school plays, or help write the newspaper, there wasn't much of anything that was going to happen.

Most wealthy people invest in a wide range of asset types and classes. They are always looking for purchases that will provide strong returns, and they will consider opportunities in many areas. And the many investors who like to concentrate on just one field usually diversify within that field. They identify a number of investments in that area and select those they feel will perform best. Though I understand this focus on one arena, and believe it works quite well, I still think it's limited in its thinking. A good wealth builder can increase opportunities many times over by diversifying outside of a specific asset type or sector.

The world will constantly change around you, and part of the investing process is in understanding that you cannot be married to any single idea. You must be prepared to stay aware, be flexible, and reallocate portions of your portfolio accordingly. For a simple example, when interest rates are low, it might be a great time to borrow, and when interest rates are high, it might be a great time to lend. When your needs and desires change, your investment strategy must adapt to follow suit and meet new conditions and demands. Flexibility is an asset and many investors will pay a premium for it. The ability to make quick, well-reasoned changes holds value and will help you to confidently take charge of your investment strategy in spite of changes that may occur.

The Team and the Knowledge

Every investment plan is different. Once you clearly communicate your current situation and objectives to your wealth-building mentor and team, you should be able to choose a strategy that resonates with you. Your main job in creating wealth is to confidently take the lead in directing your wealth plan. You cannot turn this important role over to anyone else, because no one will look after, care about, or give the attention to your investments that you will. Nor will they fully understand your investing objectives as well as you do, or have as much to lose.

In many areas, others will have greater knowledge, more experience, or better insights than you, at least at first. But you must always lead the team and lead your wealth. A good wealth-building team should have a business broker who can scout out private placement, leveraged buyout, and franchise and licensing opportunities as well as an investment banker in the deal flow, various sector analysts, and various field partners. Your field partners should include commercial and residential brokers, project scouts and managers, contractors, builders, developers, and others with tentacles that can reach out to investment opportunities ranging from oil and gas to ostrich farms, from cash equivalents to collectibles. Regardless of how well you know your brokers or field partners, it is very important to have contracts with each member of your team for each deal. Keep it all legal.

Many investing opportunities may resonate with you but not work for others. In order to lead your team most effectively, you must choose members who work best, given your investment disposition. An accountant who strongly recommends investing in stamps makes no sense to the investor who thinks stamps are for canceling, not collecting.

Due Diligence

"I don't know" doesn't play well in the world of wealth building. If you and certainty have been somewhat estranged lately, it's time to invite it back over. You need to change "I don't know" to "I'll find out" and shift limited thinking to decisive thinking. Certainty is just confidence that comes from experience and knowledge. I've heard too many people tell me that they think investing is too risky for them, before they've even studied or explored their options. There are many people who do not ski because they believe it is too risky. Yet for those of us with the skills and experience to ski, this seems a shame.

Risk can be measured, quantified, and often removed, but too often it serves as permission to be lazy with one's life and money. In fact, I think some of it is the subconscious mind saying "I don't deserve it," "It's too hard," and "I don't know." That's where I advise you to spend time with the wealth community and elicit informational interviews and conversations. If you communicate only with people who are doing the same things you're doing and achieving the same results you are— you'll stagnate.

It's time to stretch and expand your thinking. "It's too risky" is no longer permission to not try something. In building your wealth, I want to help you to redefine risk as something that has to do with experience and education more than anything else. The more you educate yourself through due diligence—that is, through research, investigation, inquiry, and exploration—the more knowledge you have about something. And the more knowledge you have about something, the less risk it seems to have. You can start by reading as much as you can about a given area of investment. Sources include investment and finance books, financial sections of the newspaper, financial and investment newsletters and magazines, and online, print, television, and radio finance and investment programs. Every world has its own language, and you'll need to start to learn the finance and investing vocabulary. For example, the language of real estate revolves around occupancy rates, local property values, current rental ranges, loan-to-value ratios, mortgage terms, and management costs. It will seem daunting at first, but once you realize it's just tribal language such as any group tends to create, you'll be deciphering the words in no time.

It's important to keep your critical eye open when conducting research. I've read articles in respected newspapers that tell people not to invest, but to save their money because in retirement they're going to have to live on less and they can't afford to take any chances. I don't know about you, but I do not want my life to narrow—I want it to expand. And to me, savings, with the ever-present potential for inflation to outrun my returns, is more risky than investing. I've also seen advisors who suggest you pay off all your consumer debt before you even think of investing. To me, that's fear-based advice that will keep you from ever creating the opportunity for your wealth to erode your debt as the Wealth Cycle does. Another great way to gain knowledge is to attend courses, lectures, workshops, and seminars. Again, you must lead your wealth by being particular about those groups or organizations to which you give your time and your ear, not to mention your entrance fee. If anyone tells you the money is going to roll in fast, let me remind you that it will probably roll out just as fast.

The next step after collecting knowledge is to conduct due diligence on every single investment you ever consider. Never skip this step. Ask any investment banker or equity analyst how he or she studies the value of a company, and due diligence will be the answer. You must do due diligence.

Traditionally, due diligence referred to the review and verification of certain details in any given deal and was usually performed by lawyers and accountants. As individuals began to make their own deals, outside of the investment banking and brokerage firm inner circle, they started to conduct their own due diligence on investments. And though you will rely on a team of accountants and lawyers to help you with your due diligence, as the leader of your wealth team, you always want to do some of the initial inquiry and research yourself. But that's not as hard as it sounds. There are plenty of people who can help you learn and perform due diligence, especially those in the industry or those who have done similar transactions. Your lawyer probably has a checklist to which you can refer, but ultimately the responsibility is always with the investor, that is, you.

Due diligence usually begins with a checklist of certain financial, operational, organizational, and sector details, but it can run a gamut of specifications, depending on the type of business and the industry in which it runs. It's not a standard checklist and usually takes some experience to compile and execute. There has never been a better time to collect information. Just a few short years ago, investment information was available only to the few who had access to the investment banks and brokerage firms through which the deals and trades were flowing. Now, thanks to the realization that the retail market of regular folks is a great source of capital, banks and other organizations are reaching out to individuals like you who are eager to generate wealth.

All forms of media, including television, radio, and print, as well as interactive platforms, such as the Internet, provide a wide reach for the banks, businesses, and idea generators to reach potential investors. Interactive platforms also provide the investor with an active channel through which to obtain information. Unfortunately, this also means that there is equal access for both good and bad opportunities to find their way to you and your money.

You must be vigilant about collecting knowledge and filtering the good from the bad, especially if you are leveraging other people's money to enhance your own investments. Though it may seem that money is the most precious thing you have to lose, your reputation is a much more valuable commodity. You can lose money over and over and still stay in the game, but if you lose one bit of your reputation the game may be over for you before it's begun. As a novice investor, you may not be able to differentiate a real deal from a bad investment idea, and that's why you have a mentor and a team to help you synthesize the information you're collecting. Elite investors engage only with this inner circle, and in your leadership role, it's your duty to make sure that you are an elite investor. There is no need for you to play in the outer circles of predators and get-rich-quick schemes. With the right information, the capacity to do due diligence, and the right support system in place, you'll make good choices.

I suggest you try this on a very small level, just to gain some real experience with this model. In many areas throughout the United States, you can buy cash flow–producing houses for as little as $6,000. Members of our Team-Made Millionaire community often hop on a plane to spend time scouting out these markets with knowledgeable field partners, so I know a lot of these opportunities exist.

Value, Growth, Income

All investors have different objectives. Some have enough cash to live on, and just want to build up net worth. Others need cash flow coming in every month. I know people who have net worth, over a million dollars of it, and because they've been trained to believe net worth is so great, they think they're set, yet they wonder why they are consumed by credit card debt. They are millionaires with no money. You can't eat your house or take off a shingle to buy a car. Most of us need cash flow. For some of us, it might be better to rent in the place we want to live and put the money into assets that can create cash flow. Sitting on one highly appreciating asset is not part of the Wealth Cycle process.

Some investors will only pursue what they see as value opportunities, and invest solely in businesses and properties that they believe have unrecognized potential and are being offered at a discount to others in their sectors. Growth investors will only play in opportunities that have consistent, above average returns, but usually also like to see the money pumped back into operations. Income investors are looking for immediate cash out in the form of rental, lease, interest, or dividends payments; they see appreciation of the asset as icing on the cake. Many investors are not aggressive, favor caution, and just want the basic level of security. Others will take more risk in the hope of more reward. Some investors will only play the opportunities the masses play, and others are open to learning about more unconventional approaches. There are those who will only buy in a specific industry or arena, or look at assets with a minimum or maximum size or valuation.

As you consider the opportunities, you must be sure that they fit in with your money rules, that is, investing criteria based on

1. Your visions, by satisfying the return on investment that will get you to your financial goals
2. Your values, so that you can still be who you are when you get to where you want to be

If you know your own requirements, it helps you to sift through the myriad of offers that will start to flow your way. Finding investment opportunities is not the problem. They will surface everywhere you look. There's probably someone with a compelling voice and a dazzling deal dialing your phone number right now. The challenge is choosing the right opportunities at the right time.

Active versus Passive Investing

In order to choose the investment strategies that are right for you, you need to determine if you want to be an active or a passive investor. Neither is better than the other, but one might appeal to you more. Though these approaches are somewhat self-explanatory, let's just make sure we're all speaking the same language.

1. The active investor has a direct involvement in the investment. The active investor may become a general partner or take roles in the management of a business or particular venture.

2. The passive investor has a passive involvement in the investment. The passive investor essentially puts up money and relies on others to do the work. Since you must always lead your Wealth Cycle, this means you monitor the progress diligently.

Surprisingly, most investors do not decide beforehand whether they wish to invest actively or passively. But if you don't make that decision, it will be made for you by default. For example, the manager of the property you own could make decisions without consulting you. Or, you could be called upon to contribute time, energy, and expertise to enterprises that you have no desire to become directly involved in.

Wealthy people usually have both types of investments, and you will probably be both a passive and an active investor. Every decision on your overall investment strategy, and on each investment, must be based on your personal objectives, values, and circumstances. There is no one-size-fits-all financial plan. Whatever your overall wealth objective, you need to select the investment strategy that gets you there in the best way. The following criteria will help you decide if you want to be an active or a passive investor:

1. Enjoyment of, and interest in, a particular niche
2. Time and energy availability and ability
3. Capacity to confront and overcome the learning curve
4. Willingness to take responsibility for the results
5. Desire to work with others on the plan
6. Willingness to cede control to others

Multiple Streams of Revenue and Entity Structuring

Most wealthy people do not invest in just one thing. They have multiple streams of revenue. And this means they have a systemized and organized structure for each. For each investment you consider, you're going to set up an entity—a business that will manage and oversee these investments. There is no getting around the fact that entities will help you accumulate more wealth. However, you cannot just create an entity because you think that it's fun to make up the names of companies. The purpose of a business is to create commerce for a business activity such as investing, product development, or a service offering.

In creating a business to focus on investing, you will create companies for each of your specific investments. This will model the habits of the wealthy, who build wealth by using assets to generate more assets. You might, for example, create an entity to start a business to fund a real estate investment. Then you might take the returns from that venture to invest in another company you run, one that invests in oil and gas. In the process, you will diversify your portfolio and end up with many legal entities that own your investments. By creating your own company or companies, you are contributing to your Wealth Cycle and helping to form the foundation to generate assets that will accelerate that Wealth Cycle. This is the new way, a strategy to forecast and move toward a Financial Freedom Day that will come sooner, and last longer, and be bigger and better than any budgeting to retirement plan could ever offer.

Asset Allocation

Too many people believe that if they buy stocks through a broker they are investing for their wealth. Last I looked, the stock market was generating single-digit, sometimes low-double-digit, returns. That's interesting, but not helpful. Though I do own several stocks, stocks I manage myself and not through a broker, I also like to look at who else wants my money and how much they're willing to pay for it. It seems to me that the possibilities for participating in profit potential are infinite.

I could choose to own a $40,000 house in the middle of the country that spits out $2,000 a year in cash flow, or own a deed in an oil head that's going to give me 25 percent return on my investment, or participate in a vitamin manufacturing plant and watch 48 percent of my money come back in the first year. These are just some of my investments, direct investments I made into assets, without paying fees and commissions or giving up control to someone sitting behind a bank of computers. I like managing my own wealth; it's just too much fun. It gives me a sense of security, control, and responsibility. Of course, you will not start at these high numbers. When people start to invest, their money sits in the Wealth Account generating 1 to 3 percent returns. Then, they ramp it up to ROIs of 10, 20, 30 percent and beyond. I'm in projects that have 50 percent returns for which I've put no money or credit down. But those kinds of deals do not come to beginners.

When you look at investments you need to do so from the perspective of having income goals and asset goals, depending on whether your objective is to create net worth or cash flow. You should also decided how much money you want to make this year, how much you can invest, and then, based on potential returns, how you will invest it. This is all about self-direction and being creative about opportunities. The number one way to do a deal, though, is to have a plan. You need to get organized; then you can play. Most people with whom you play, who are putting deals together, want others in their deal, but only if these others have their own plan. Everyone on a team has to be responsible for him- or herself. If you cherry-pick your deals based on the appeal of the deal and those doing it, rather than choosing deals that strategically fit into your asset plan, you will end up with a hodgepodge of assets that don't make sense.

Direct diversified asset allocation is a slow, but sure, systematic approach. It takes time, and it happens over time. You move with decisive care, but also act with swiftness when necessary. When things are bad, you get out. We're not doing park-and-pray—you are in control. Give it a "Wasn't that interesting?" and move on to something else. This is an overview of the concept of direct asset allocation, and in no way reflects my portfolio or suggests one I think you should have. Investing is very personal, and only you know which assets match up with your financial objectives and values. I have some partners in my community who invest in some of the above and others who invest in none of the above. We even have some folks who look at assets completely outside of these categories, such as accounts receivable factoring, mobile homes, and tax-lien certificates. There is a bounty of asset opportunities. With research, you will discover them.

I believe that an optimal Wealth Cycle is built on an asset alloca-tion strategy that contains a diverse blend of assets. If you create a diverse portfolio, you won't be married to any single investment type, so your purchases will be based on potential returns and less influenced by subjective factors. In addition, if you diversify, you won't be as badly burnt when a particular category spins into a bad cycle, as most investments are likely to do. And I can't say it enough: to control a diverse portfolio you must lead your wealth team. It's essential for you to work with others because you cannot do it all expertly yourself.

Creating the Bucket of Risk and Reward

How you diversify your assets is a decision that will depend on you and your situation. I'm often asked how diverse a portfolio should be and what that diversity looks like. Because I favor more nontra-ditional assets, I'd consider the following to be good diversification strategies.

	REAL ESTATE	STOCKS	OIL & GAS	CASH	BUSINESSES
A	30%	20%	10%	10%	30%
B	60%	20%	10%	10%	—
C	20%	50%	—	5%	25%

Again, your preferences will depend on you, as well as on the in-fluence and backgrounds of the mentors you choose. A top-notch wealth team will help you to look at all your options and get the ex-pert help and advice you need. But it starts with you. You might work with the most talented investors in the world, but you still need to be reading the books, the magazines, and the newspapers and collecting all the general and specific information you can in order to best lead your wealth team. Given that risk is aligned with education and experience, smart investors are well-educated about the marketplace and stay connected to their communities. They can read the numbers, and they know what constitutes a good investment. For real estate investments, savvy investors look at the numbers first, and if they check out, they then look at the property.

Making your wealth grow is an educational process. As you build wealth, you will develop new understanding and learn how to vary your strategy according to the investment climate and your particular needs and circumstances. When it comes to risk, remember these rules:

1. **Enhance opportunity.** Whenever possible, operate with other people's money (OPM) and spend as little of your own as you can. We also recommend using other people's credit (OPC). Get knowledge and experience on your team so as to reduce risk for everyone involved, and do not take reckless gambles.

2. **Know the market.** Educate yourself about a market so that you can be strategic in that market. Study, get advice, and create action so that you can gain experience and evidence. But realize that each opportunity is different. For example, investing in oil and gas takes patience. Some of these investments can take anywhere from 18 months to 5 years to start bringing in money, but once they do, the returns can be stunning.

3. **Specialize.** Become an expert in specific investment areas and specialize within those areas. Learn how to diversify your investments in these fields. Again, I believe you can learn about many fields, but only you know your capacity to absorb and use a range of information.

4. **Watch the details.** Always maintain detailed and complete records.
5. **Do the math.** Treat numbers as your friend, not your foe. Understand how to read and calculate numbers to analyze investment opportunities. Like everything else in the investing field, the numbers are not that complicated once you learn what they represent and gain experience using them.
6. **Follow the rules.** Stick to the money rules you've established.
7. **Listen, learn, and lead.** Communicate well with your mentors, your wealth team, and your asset-specific experts. Utilize all the resources around you and gain conviction in your decision making.

As you build your empire of entities, whether they are businesses for your investments in other people's assets or your own, you should think about what you want your Wealth Cycle to look like. This means defining the asset allocation.

Consider Real Estate

I tell people to buy real estate to learn how to run a business, set up entities, and diversify their assets, as well as reap some immediate cash flow, depreciation, and tax deductions. Real estate is a slow game, and I recommend you first create a real estate business that will then become your investment. While it is absolutely possible to create tens of thousands of dollars of passive income per month and a net worth of hundreds of thousands of dollars, you need to have a real estate management action plan in place and be very clear on your financial goals and goal achievement investment plans.

Many real estate owners and investors begin in their own back-yards and suggest others do the same. Given that I live on the water and escape to another home in the mountains, I believe you should live where you want but invest where it makes sense. In only a few short years, I have developed a diverse portfolio of real estate assets in several states. This, though, works only if you believe in the Team-Made Millionaire approach, because it takes a network of field partners around the country to make it work. Field partners are the professionals in the streets who know the real estate and the opportunities. The benefit of national real estate is that by investing with field partners you get inside information as if you are in your own backyard, but you also diversify your risk, you leverage a variety of market economies, and you strategically partner with teams with a vested interest in the performance of the properties. Additionally, I recommend learning how to leverage your own money with OPM—other people's money. Leverage is a great route to success in real estate and in all investments. In addition to other people's money, you should also try to garner other people's creativity, knowledge, connections, know-how, time, and resources.

In real estate, as with all asset opportunities, you need to get a mentor, get a team, and get your know-how before you get on with it. Doing real estate right or doing it wrong can be the difference between a happy day and a very sad one. Though it may seem exciting and productive to buy real estate, holding assets without an entity plan or financial strategy in place could be detrimental to your broad objective. I knew a guy who owned 34 houses and held all of them as rentals. He'd reached the point where he was losing a lot of money and the banks wouldn't lend him any more. The houses were all in his name and his tax situation was untenable. I worked with him to reverse his financial situation. First, we talked about his psychology about money and exposed him to the idea of working with others to buy and invest in real estate. He needed to understand that if he had good deals, then using other people's money was good for him and good for the other people and their money. Second, we took everything out of his name and helped him create several separate LLCs that owned the properties and an S corporation that managed them. As a result of creating entities and using OPM, he was able to borrow again, double the houses he owned, and see his colleagues get returns of 8 to 10 percent on their investments. He continues to use OPM and bank debt to purchase a dozen or so houses at a time.

There are a variety of opportunities in real estate, some bigger games than others, but as your experience grows, so can your game. You can consider land development, preconstruction, and preforeclosures. Preforeclosures are a good example of how you can make the pie bigger for everyone. Foreclosures are worse than bankruptcy and not something anyone should endure if they can avoid it. We have a field partner in a small town down south who knows almost everything that's going on with everyone. When we hooked up with her, she was the one to call if you were having trouble with finances and were worried about losing your home. We watched as she sat in the kitchens of these frustrated folks and talked with them over coffee. She was transparent and candid as she explained that it was a good investment and a profitable venture for her to help them repair their credit and keep them away from bankruptcy by paying them a fair price for the equity in their house and taking over their mortgage. Time and again, this was perceived as the biggest gift they'd ever received. They were free to figure it out again, with money in hand and debt off their backs.

For all the reasons I mentioned, including depreciation and the real cash flow I receive monthly, real estate is one of my favorite investments. Though I've lost money on several properties, and I continue to learn as I play in this field, overall I've done very well. There's even a mortgage lender on my wealth team who used to make $52,000 a year who now makes that much in a month. There's no better team exercise than real estate, simply because it requires so much expertise and legwork. But it's a great arena in which to underscore the fact that you don't have to do all that legwork—you just need to lead it.

The Opportunity for IRAs

Though the money you've locked away in savings, through IRAs, pensions, Social Security and other withholding plans, must remain out of your hands, there are ways to create even more wealth using IRAs. In recent years, self-directed IRA plans have blossomed. As I mentioned in Chapter 3, there are many self-directed IRAs at large brokerage firms, but only a handful of True Self-Directed IRA companies that will support the type of asset allocation we're doing here. As you can guess, since I encourage you to manage your own wealth, I strongly suggest you move your IRA over to a True Self-Directed IRA. Tax-deferred IRA money, or preferably a tax-free Roth IRA, can accelerate your wealth accumulation. By using your Roth IRA to invest in assets, you allow your money to build up on a tax-deferred basis and then withdraw it tax-free.

With True Self-Directed IRA plans you can invest directly in assets, not just mutual funds, REITs, or other indirect vehicles to participation. You can also partner with your IRA and put together investment plans where both you and your IRA benefit. For example, if your IRA participates in the purchase of a rental property, not only does a portion of the monthly cash flow go back into the IRA, but the IRA can pay all the fees on the house, such as taxes, because incoming expenses flow to ownership. I've also seen people use IRAs in oil and gas deals, accounts receivable factoring, and a variety of assets. IRAs can also create a note and lend other people money, providing the IRA with interest payments that are, again, tax-free. You should also scout about for other tax-free opportunities: for example, if you invest in educational savings accounts, you can pay for your children's schooling with pretax dollars. For information on these and True Self-Directed IRAs, see the Resources at the back of the book.

Back to Rick's Wealth Plan

The next building block in Rick Noonan's Wealth Cycle Process was *Entities*. For Rick's assets we set up several entities:

- An LLC for his real estate properties
- An LLC for his start-up company investment
- An LLC for his four preconstruction houses
- An S corporation for his business
- A trust to serve as an umbrella for all his companies and holdings

We would also consider a C corporation when Rick's businesses grow, a strategy discussed in Chapter 6.

Forecasting was the next building block. A little expense management could do wonders for Rick's life. We set him up with a chart of accounts.

	PERSONAL	LLC REAL ESTATE	LLC START-UP	LLC PRE-CONSTRUCTION	S CORP. MARKETING	TOTAL
REVENUE						
EXPENDITURES						
ASSETS						
LIABILITIES						

Rick would need to stay on top of this process by coding each expense as he spent, so that he would drive his expenses for the bookkeeper he would need to engage.

Though direct asset allocation was Rick's first step in activating his Wealth Cycle Process, the real acceleration of his Wealth Cycle, through increased asset allocation, couldn't really begin until several other building blocks were in place, such as his entities, his Cash Machine, and, of course, the Wealth Account. If Rick were to try to accelerate his Wealth Cycle without getting his Wealth Account in place, he'd be building on a foundation that wasn't solid, and his acceleration would falter. He might be able to spot deals and opportunities, and even close a few, but if his source of cash—his Wealth Account—was not up and running, his options would be severely limited and he'd miss out on great investment opportunities. Even worse, he might see his financial foundation crumble beneath him.

For Rick, the *Wealth Account* step was critical. Without the Wealth Account, all his money would most likely have flown right back out in the form of taxes or expenditures. Rick's Wealth Account was going to feed his Wealth Cycle and keep that money cycling into more money, forever.

The *Cash Machine* was the next building block for Rick. Getting a man committed to the commute to quit his job is nearly as much fun as pulling gum out of my kid's hair. Rick Noonan had been a company man for years. The idea of venturing out into his own business did not appeal to him.

"I wouldn't mind doing my own business if it was an investment fund, like owning real estate," Rick said.

"Well, that's interesting, but not helpful, Rick. We need you to learn to earn by using skills you already have, in an industry you already know. You've got to learn how to run a business. Once you know how to do that, you can have a business in any arena you want. You need a Cash Machine that will immediately generate revenue to accelerate your Wealth Cycle. You're going to create a marketing firm."

"I don't want to help people market."

"Fine," I said. "Even better. You know other marketers and brand professionals, probably some who don't have jobs right now or are retired and looking for something to do?" He nodded. "Great," I said. "You'll hire some marketing and brand management professionals you know to work with other businesses so that you can learn how to run a business without having to do any of the actual service yourself. You just need to learn how to market the concept and build a company."

"I'll try it," he said, shaking his head.

"You'll use the $10,000 in cash you have to pay for setting up the business and finding clients. Let's give it two months to ramp up. And let's see if we can make you a $250,000 business in the first year. That would mean six clients, each of whom needs 20 hours of marketing assistance a month. If you charge $200 an hour for those 20 hours, that's $4,000 per client per month, which gets us to $24,000 a month gross revenue. If you pay your contractors half, that's $12,000 a month in pretax income to you."

ONE-YEAR FREEDOM DAY GOALS

REVENUE	**ASSETS**
CASH MACHINE	
MARKETING FIRM: $12,000/month in pretax income, after two-month ramp-up to six clients	Use $10,000 in cash for start-up costs
PASSIVE INCOME	
$6,400/month cash flow from ➝	$270,000 shift of assets into real estate, business

FINANCIAL BASELINE

PRETAX INCOME: $12,500/month   **ASSETS:** $490,000

EXPENDITURES: $7,000/month   **LIABILITIES:** $85,000

SKILL SET: Marketing, brand management

If Rick could nail his marketing strategy and get clients, his Cash Machine could be a $250,000 business that potentially generated $120,000 of pretax income in the first 10 months of business after paying his contractors. Plus, the Cash Machine gave Rick another business against which to manage his expenses and his tax strategy. I also suggested that Rick put $1,000 a month from the business into three separate educational savings accounts to fund his children's college tuition, for a total of $3,000 a month.

Finally, we focused on *Debt Management*. Rick's mortgage was at a low 5 percent interest rate leveraged against a continuously appreciating asset. We were going to leave that alone. Rick had no credit card debt, and I would just suggest to him that he continue to manage this process in the way he'd been doing.

Now it was time for Rick to lead his wealth—to fully incorporate the *Leadership* building block. Because Rick was already making a good salary and had shifted some assets to create a nice bit of passive income, keeping up the momentum would be his biggest challenge.

Conditioning was a key factor in how Rick would manage his Wealth Cycle. Rick's father had worked for a company his whole life and Rick was comfortable with that model, and so was his wife. His courageous shifting of assets was already the subject of a difficult conversation with his wife, but it was a good thing that Rick and his wife were now having these conversations. However, for Rick to (1) take advantage of the depreciation of his real estate, (2) better utilize the $50,000 sitting in his company's stock, and (3) lead and build his team and generally focus more time and attention on his Wealth Cycle, he was going to have to leave his job.

To make him more comfortable with this inevitability and manage his Wealth Cycle properly, Rick needed *Teamwork*. He needed a coach to help him create a weath plan, a mentor to support him in the process, field partners in oil and gas, real estate, and small businesses to find those direct and diversified asset allocation opportunities, a CPA who understood entity structuring, a bookkeeper to help with the forecasting, a good lawyer for the paperwork, and a supportive wife. The man was going to be immersed in the world of team building.

Taking Charge

Without leaving his job, Rick now had the capacity to create $18,400 a month in additional revenue as well as build his net worth—a task accomplished by just a quick shifting of assets and the infusion of a Cash Machine. With the entity structure and Wealth Account in place, Rick would be in a position to retain and recycle a lot of that income to accelerate his Wealth Cycle. The Wealth Cycle can't be inactive. In order to flourish, it must grow, and this means more and more streams of income must feed it. As we saw with the Leonard family and now with Rick, one great source of fuel to accelerate the Wealth Cycle is a legitimate business venture—soon to be the Cash Machine.

Activation is good, acceleration is better . . .

5

THE CASH MACHINE
Learn to Earn

In the Wealth Cycle Process, it's imperative to have a Cash Machine. To do this, you must move out of our permission-based society and make it happen. There's no longer room for you to wait for someone to give you more money. You can increase your income by improving the business you currently have or by starting a new venture. Now wait, stop, don't protest yet. I know that this may sound like a deal breaker, but I assure you, it isn't. I'm talking about a business venture that works comfortably with a skill set you already have. In fact, of the many definitions of wealth I've heard over the years, the one I like best defines wealth as "the act of profuse abundance through the actualization of one's skills and gifts." I believe you can and should use your skills to make money.

Our goal is to take those skills and gifts you have and put you in immediate action so that you can learn a whole new skill set, that of running your own business. Then, when you do become wealthy, you will have the business skills—marketing, sales, operations, management, and so forth—to run your life, which will look a lot like a business, and to create a business for any widget that winds its way out of your brain. For those of you who already have a business, we'll make sure we get that business revved up so that you are a true marketing machine, generating revenues and creating cash. Here's the sequence:

1. Use a known skill set.
2. Create a viable Cash Machine.
3. Learn business skills.
4. Take those business skills into any arena you desire.

In this book I am going to teach you how to earn. This will not take over your life; the initial goal is just to create a small venture that will grow slowly. Like the Leonard family, it might already be a hobby that we'll formalize and develop into a Cash Machine.

Own Your Outcome

I met Patricia Beasley during a Team-Made Millionaire seminar in Philadelphia. Patricia was 40, divorced, and the mother of a teenage daughter. A project manager for a Web design firm, making $45,000 a year, Patricia was eager to start her own summer camp. She came to the Team-Made Millionaire seminar hoping I'd show her the way. I showed her the way all right—which was away from owning her own summer camp—for now. That was the right move but at the wrong time.

As you've seen in each Gap Analysis, the Wealth Cycle Process requires both passive income from assets and money from a business venture, that is, the Cash Machine, to sustain and continuously accelerate wealth. The Entities and Forecasting chapters will describe the multiple tax advantages open to you once you have established your own business. And as far as direct investing goes, there can be no better direct investment than yourself and your vision. Your wealth will come from multiple streams of income, and one of them should be your own business.

Bring Your Brain

Though many people understand that a key catalyst to creating more wealth is to make more money, most people tell me they have no idea how to do that. Most of us were exposed to some aspect of the working world growing up, but most of us never learned how to earn. In considering your options for a Cash Machine, you may have some big-dream, pie-in-the sky vision. And although I think you should make it a goal to eventually create a wonderful business venture, when I talk about you starting your own business, I'm not talking about that. Not yet. You get to do what you like only after you make money and gain business skills doing what you already know. If you've never owned or managed a business before, chances are that your skill set is quite limited. You just don't have the experience. I strongly recommend that you start your first business in an area you are very familiar with. Then you can take the skills that you've learned into the field of your dreams.

Patricia Beasley's Wealth Plan

Patricia Beasley answered my eight questions in eight minutes flat.

Question 1: What Is Your Monthly Income?

"Whatever $45,000 divided by 12 is," she said.

ONE-YEAR FREEDOM DAY GOALS	
REVENUE	*ASSETS*
FINANCIAL BASELINE	
(*PRETAX INCOME: $3,750/month*)	*ASSETS:*
EXPENDITURES:	*LIABILITIES:*
SKILL SET:	

Question 2: What Are Your Monthly Expenditures?

"Whatever a bit more than $45,000 divided by 12 is," she said.

One of the first steps I knew I'd have to take with Patricia would be to clean up her approach to her financials. People with sloppy personal financial habits have sloppy business habits.

"No, it's more like $2,000 a month," she said quickly.

ONE-YEAR FREEDOM DAY GOALS

REVENUE	ASSETS
FINANCIAL BASELINE	
PRETAX INCOME: *$3,750/month*	ASSETS:
(EXPENDITURES: *$2,000/month*)	LIABILITIES:
SKILL SET:	

Question 3: What Assets Do You Have?

"I have $80,000 in a 401(k) at my current job and $5,000 in savings," she said. "That's it. I rent my apartment."

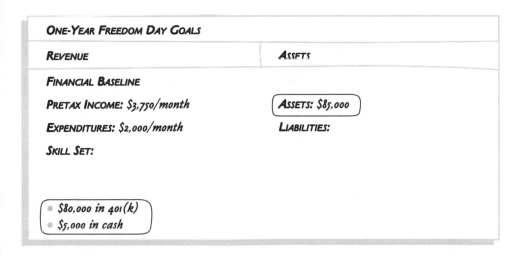

ONE-YEAR FREEDOM DAY GOALS

REVENUE	ASSETS
FINANCIAL BASELINE	
PRETAX INCOME: *$3,750/month*	(ASSETS: *$85,000*)
EXPENDITURES: *$2,000/month*	LIABILITIES:
SKILL SET:	

- *$80,000 in 401(k)*
- *$5,000 in cash*

Question 4: What Are Your Liabilities?

"I have $10,000 in credit card debt and growing, I'm sure," she said.

ONE-YEAR FREEDOM DAY GOALS	
REVENUE	*ASSETS*
FINANCIAL BASELINE	
PRETAX INCOME: $3,750/month	*ASSETS: $85,000*
EXPENDITURES: $2,000/month	*LIABILITIES: $10,000*
SKILL SET:	
• *$10,000 credit card debt*	

Question 5: What Else?

"That's it, really."

"Any IRAs?"

"Who?"

She was serious. I shook my head and went to my sixth question.

Question 6: What Do You Want?

"I'd like $10 million and $200,000 a month in cash flow."

"You're on Fantasy Island," I said.

To say that her gap from Financial Baseline to Freedom Day was huge would be an understatement. We talked about lowering her one-year Freedom Day goal to an objective that would still create tension and inspire her to move ahead, but that wouldn't feel so daunting that she might quit. She agreed to readjust.

"But I still have my vision to run a summer camp," Patricia said. "A nonprofit, for underprivileged kids," she said, almost in a nervous whisper.

"Stunning," I said. "Now let's bring some reality to your Fantasy Island."

Though it may not seem so, I was very supportive of Patricia's desire to create the nonprofit summer camp. In fact, I'm the founding board member of Life-School, an outdoor youth education program with a similar vision. I believe a huge part of wealth building is philanthropy. Creating your own success and helping others is the most rewarding venture. And if you create communities of people who also believe you have to give to get, you keep the circle around you filled with genuine and sincere people. But if Patricia pursued her nonprofit summer camp before she had her own feet on the ground, they'd both sink. She had the right idea—she just wasn't ready for it. Patricia needed to find her sequencing and do the right thing at the right time. I knew I couldn't get Patricia to $10 million in one year. I'm into steady and sure wealth building that's sustained, not get-rich-quick schemes that evaporate as quickly as they are produced. But I also knew we could change her life and get her well on her way. We wrote in her new, more realistic goals.

ONE-YEAR FREEDOM DAY GOALS
- *Create profitable business*
- *Get out of debt*
- *Establish a college fund for her daughter*
- *Provide $2,000/month of passive income*

REVENUE	ASSETS
FINANCIAL BASELINE	
PRETAX INCOME: *$3,750/month*	**ASSETS:** *$85,000*
EXPENDITURES: *$2,000/month*	**LIABILITIES:** *$10,000*
SKILL SET:	

Question 7: What Skills Do You Use to Make Money?

"I'm a project manager, so I oversee the design guys and the technical guys at a Web design firm. I drive traffic, organize, administrate, and I'm fluent in techie talk."

ONE-YEAR FREEDOM DAY GOALS
- *Create profitable business*
- *Get out of debt*
- *Establish a college fund for her daughter*
- *Provide $2,000/month of passive income*

REVENUE	*ASSETS*
FINANCIAL BASELINE	
PRETAX INCOME: $3,750/month	*ASSETS: $85,000*
EXPENDITURES: $2,000/month	*LIABILITIES: $10,000*
SKILL SET: Project management, Web design	

Question 8: Are You Willing to Create and Execute the Wealth Cycle Process?

Gap Analysis   Leadership

"Yes," Patricia said.

"Yes is the right answer," I said.

Following the eight questions in eight minutes, Patricia's Gap Analysis looked like this:

ONE-YEAR FREEDOM DAY GOALS
- *Create profitable business*
- *Get out of debt*
- *Establish a college fund for her daughter*
- *Provide $2,000/month of passive income*

REVENUE   **ASSETS**

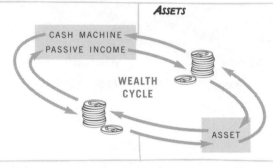

FINANCIAL BASELINE

PRETAX INCOME: $3,750/month   *ASSETS: $85,000*

EXPENDITURES: $2,000/month   *LIABILITIES: $10,000*

SKILL SET: Project management, Web design

- *$80,000 in 401(k)*
- *$5,000 in cash*
- *$10,000 credit card debt*

With no assets available to invest and no huge source of income, I saw the building blocks of Patricia Beasley's Wealth Cycle sequence in this way:

Gap Analysis → Financial Baseline → Freedom Day

Cash Machine → Entities → Forecasting →
Wealth Account → Assets → Debt Management

Leadership + Conditioning + Teamwork

Patricia Beasley's Wealth Plan

The first building block for Patricia in the Wealth Cycle Process was the *Gap Analysis*. In Patricia's Gap Analysis we uncovered a woman with a lot of ambition but no tangible resources. It seemed to me that Patricia needed to create some money fast. In order for us to get our hands on some of that $80,000 in the 401(k), Patricia would have to quit her job. She shook her head. No, she couldn't quit. "My daughter's at that age where she wants a new pair of jeans every month."

"Let's get your daughter involved in your business so that she can buy her own jeans," I said. "And you can build the business even bigger."

Next came the *Financial Baseline*. Patricia's income was short of her expenditures, her credit card debt had to go, and her assets were tied up in qualified money. We were going to have to shake things up a bit. As it is with almost every Wealth Cycle Process, Patricia's Wealth Account was going to work in tandem with her Debt Management. We were both eager to get Patricia into the Five-Step Debt Elimination Plan and establish her Wealth Account as aggressively as possible. We were going to make sure that Patricia's wealth would spiral up while her debt spiraled down.

Patricia's *Freedom Day* was based on a realistic, but still motivating goal, and I could see a wealth plan that within one year would get her to

- ☞ Create a profitable business
- ☞ Get out of debt
- ☞ Establish a college fund for her daughter
- ☞ Earn $2,000/month of passive income

Her daughter, presumably working in the business too, would also have her own one-year Freedom Day goal in the form of an educational savings account.

I also thought Patricia's desire to own and run a summer camp was a worthwhile vision, and I was eager to help her achieve it.

In order to kick off the Wealth Cycle Process, we needed to start with the Cash Machine building block; Patricia needed to make more money. Patricia's skills prompted me to suggest that she create a Web design firm as her Cash Machine. In order for Patricia to learn how to earn, she needed to use the knowledge and skills she'd learned and the relationships she'd built as a project manager at the Web design firm to start her own Web business. Though she found the idea unappealing, and seemingly off track from her vision of a summer camp, it would enable her to bridge the gap from business know-nothing to business know-how.

The business has to be real, not some esoteric dream, so that you can establish a working Cash Machine while gaining valuable experience. For example, a teacher should start a tutoring company, a computer programmer should start an IT business, and a school counselor should start a family and marriage therapy practice. When I left a large corporation and then returned to them as a consultant, I made three times what I was making as a salaried employee. By the way, to show the reluctant among you that you are not alone, I waited until I was fully vested to leave that company. That wasn't just because I don't like to leave money on the table; it reflected remnants of my scarcity conditioning.

You must first hone those skills required of a business owner, such as marketing, sales, finance, operations, and management, before you can establish the company of your dreams. Whatever you do decide, your first business

1. Should have a low barrier to entry. That is, you should be able to have it up and running and possibly generating real money within 24 hours.
2. Shouldn't take more time than you can allot, though perhaps you can get up an hour earlier every day.
3. Shouldn't take more of your capacity than you can allot, though it will be a stretch.
4. Should diversify your income.
5. Should give you a nice return on your investment.

If you have a job right now that you are not willing to relinquish, I understand. But you need to consider a transitional plan, a bridge out of your job and into the management of your empire of entities and your multiple streams of revenue. It may surprise you, but I actually do not believe that if you do what you love, the money will follow. Ask any poet how that's going for him or her, and I'm sure you'll be hit up for a loan. I think it's important to hold onto your day job until you can establish a formidable flow of cash from your Wealth Cycle.

Just Say Yes and Figure It Out

Your skill set is the obvious place to look when brainstorming ideas for a Cash Machine. And these are not restricted to just those skills you've most recently used. For example, if you worked as a babysitter when you were younger, you could consider a business around day care. One of the clients I mentioned in the introduction, the receptionist at the law firm who created the successful dog-walking business, didn't think she had any skill sets she could convert to a business. Then she recalled that during college she had worked in a veterinary hospital and that she felt comfortable around animals.

I also suggest that people look at the market and see what other suppliers have to offer, what distinctions are being valued and what's missing. I created my coaching business when I noticed that financial education speakers were not providing any follow-up support after their seminars. Ultimately we established the idea of financial coaching in its formal, intense state. Eventually, we became the speakers. But it was the coaching skill set and this gap in the industry, the lack of postseminar support, that helped me begin my business. Additionally, I always recommend that my clients think in volume when they're starting a business. It's best to build it once and sell it many times, so always think in group volume, not individual volume. Individual volume is exhausting. A Cash Machine idea that targets a group, such as the AARP and its database of clients, rather than every person over 55, is going to be a much more profitable and efficient venture. Joint ventures with others already doing a similar or complementary business are also great inroads to establishing your Cash Machine.

Committed to the Commute

An approach I believe is unproductive is to set up entities and begin the Wealth Cycle but fail to completely transition from your job so you can focus completely on the new venture. People who do this are straddlers who want to hang onto their secure job-with-benefits package, even though their passive income would really build momentum if they gave it more of their time and attention. At this point, these day jobs do not offer safety and security so much as they represent missed time and opportunity. Even after Rick Noonan started to invest and manage his assets, he remained a classic straddler, committed to the commute and his indentured servitude.

The Business Directive

When establishing your business, you must first create a business directive. This will help you map out the sequence of steps needed to launch the business and create a presentation for possible financing. The directive should include

1. Your vision for this business
2. The business strategies and tactics employed
3. A revenue model
4. Revenue projections
5. A marketing plan
6. Sales strategies
7. Your leadership approach

There are numerous business references for helping you do this. Some are listed in the Resources section. This exercise will not only help you bridge the gap from your current to your potential skill set, but it will serve as good practice for the time when you establish your ultimate business, the one that represents your bigger vision.

Patricia wanted to make money fast so that she could get to her summer camp. But I needed her to agree to two things before she even began: to make the effort to create the Web business and to maintain her current lifestyle, keeping expenditures where they were. When I started my first coaching business, I had some money, but not enough to launch a business, and I didn't want to go into debt. I made the decision to sell everything I owned except my jeep and my computer. That first year, my goal was to just replace my salary from the job I'd left. I rented a room to have a little office. I lived with friends, paying little rent. And I earned my goal revenue in eight months.

Revving Up the Cash Machine

Revenue Modeling

Revenue modeling will help you determine if your efforts will see any reward.

"Let's see if you could do $100,000 in sales in one year," I said to Patricia. Her jaw dropped, but I started to do the math. Sometimes, the numbers aren't that daunting when you break them down. "If I took $100,000 a year and broke that number down into months, that's $8,333, which over 20 days a month is $419 a day. If you could charge $100 an hour and find work for four hours a day, that's $400."

"That does seem more manageable than $100,000 a year," Patricia said.

Just to be clear, a $100,000 business is not the goal. To run a $100,000 business for the rest of your life won't get you to your Freedom Day; you might as well keep your regular job. If you're going to be a wealth builder, you need your Cash Machine to go past a $1 million business and have others working for you. Then you'll really accelerate the Wealth Cycle. Patricia needed to focus on finding the personnel and the customers to support 20 hours of work a week at $100 an hour. This would give her $100,000 in gross sales her first year in business.

Don't Reinvent the Wheel

See who else is doing what you are doing. Chances are, someone has done 99 percent of what you want to do, so be a good researcher, find out how he or she is doing it and implement similar tactics. You may even want to look through the Yellow Pages for a competing business and visit it for advice. If you do this, make sure you pick one in a region far enough away from you so that you don't encroach on their market. They may be a good source of referrals later.

Hire Help

In instances where you can pay people to do the work rather than give them equity, pay them. Ownership of your cash machine is precious.

Marketing

Where I see most entrepreneurs fail is in marketing their business. They don't know how to get the word out. Or if they do, they stop once they get some clients or customers and fail to fill the pipeline. Marketing usually takes time to rally interest from the target audience, and then once the audience comes through the door, you've got to keep those customers, and others, coming in. Sending out blast e-mails and creating her own compelling Web site, Patricia marketed herself as a quick-turnaround, edgy design firm. She jumped on the connections she had in the Web design field and introduced herself to a whole new sector by hiring her daughter to reach out to the younger demographic of both contractors and customers. Patricia's guerrilla marketing tactics allowed her to have nominal start-up costs.

Selling

Bringing home the business and asking for the cash is key. I see great marketing efforts where the marketers get the body in the door, but then there is no one there to seal the deal once they are inside.

Best Use of Time

I've noticed that for the business owners who can't seem to make a buck, it's usually one of two things. Either their companies are structured poorly, with everything that comes in going right back out again in taxes, or they just don't know how to create more sales. This is where leadership becomes imperative. Most business owners do everything themselves, but in order for the business to grow, you must delegate. No one is ever going to do it like you do, or be as good as you are. Balls will get dropped, and so you need to train your team to drop the right balls. There's not enough of you to go around. If the task you're doing at the time is not the highest, best use of your time, then it's not the right task. In trying to make money, your number one goal is marketing. You need to find orders, create customers, and keep those customers coming back for more.

I had a client who was working on a business idea for a year. Each time I asked to see her progress, she'd show me some colorful brochure or pricing sheet. And each time I asked her how much money she was making from her business that day, her answer was zero. "But isn't this brochure beautiful?" she asked. The Wealth Cycle Process is not about great ideas or beautiful brochures. It's about getting out on the street and making more money, as soon as possible. Once you've started a business and learned the business skill set, you can start the process of pursuing your bigger vision. If you don't have a vision for a business, but you want to run one, you can learn about franchise, licensing, or network marketing opportunities that might interest you.

With a five-month ramp-up, Patricia's Web design firm would begin to add $8,000 a month of cash flow to her Wealth Cycle. After earmarking a monthly portion to her Wealth Account, her Debt Management, and her daughter's educational savings account, Pa-

ONE-YEAR FREEDOM DAY GOALS
- *Create profitable business*
- *Get out of debt*
- *Establish a college fund for her daughter*
- *Provide $2,000/month of passive income*

REVENUE

> **CASH MACHINE**
>
> *Web design firm: $8,000 cash flow/month after five-month ramp-up*

PASSIVE INCOME

ASSETS

FINANCIAL BASELINE

PRETAX INCOME: *$3,750/month*

EXPENDITURES: *$2,000/month*

SKILL SET: *Project management, Web design*

ASSETS: *$85,000*

LIABILITIES: *$10,000*

- *$80,000 in 401(k)*
- *$5,000 in cash*
- *$10,000 credit card debt*

tricia would reach her one-year Freedom Day goal of $2,000 a month of passive income.

The next building block in Patricia's Wealth Cycle Process was *Entities.* We set up an LLC for Patricia's Web design firm. Eventually, she'd have an entity for her investments and her summer camp.

In *Forecasting,* it was clear that Patricia's new business venture was going to alleviate a lot of her red ink. Not only would her Cash Machine increase her revenue, but she'd also have a legitimate business against which to code her expenditures.

	PERSONAL	LLC WEB DESIGN	TOTAL
REVENUE			
EXPENDITURES			
ASSETS			
LIABILITIES			

By spending with some financial consciousness, Patricia would develop her business, create more cash to pay off her debt, and give her Wealth Cycle a better chance to succeed

The next step was setting up Patricia's *Wealth Account.* We immediately set up two: one for Patricia's personal account and one as a holding account in her LLC. She began making the Wealth Account Priority Payment of $100 a month into each. I also encouraged her to reduce the amount of her contribution to her current employer's 401(k) and use that additional money to accelerate her Wealth Accounts. As Patricia's business grew and she retained more cash from her revenue, she was able to increase the WAPP to $1,000 a month in each account.

For the next building block, *Assets,* Patricia had $85,000, consisting of

- $80,000 in a 401(k)
- $5,000 in cash

Motivated by her vision for the summer camp, Patricia worked hard to get clients for her Web design company. In six months she had collected $3,000 in her personal Wealth Account and put another $3,000 in her business's holding account, a corporate Wealth Account that could begin generating assets.

Since she was still working in her job, Patricia couldn't touch the 401(k). But she was willing to

1. Take $1,000 from her cash account
2. Use the $3,000 from her personal Wealth Account
3. Partner with her LLC and use the $3,000 in that holding account

This came to a total of $7,000, which could then be directly allocated into assets.

ONE-YEAR FREEDOM DAY GOALS
- *Create profitable business*
- *Get out of debt*
- *Establish a college fund for her daughter*
- *Provide $2,000/month of passive income*

REVENUE

CASH MACHINE

Web design firm

PASSIVE INCOME

CASH FLOW:

$150/month cash flow from real estate property

ASSETS

SHIFT ASSETS OF $7,000:

$7,000 to real estate for one cash-flow-producing, and possibly appreciating, rental property

FINANCIAL BASELINE

PRETAX INCOME: *$3,750/month*

EXPENDITURES: *$2,000/month*

SKILL SET: *Project management, Web design*

ASSETS: *$85,000*

LIABILITIES: *$10,000*

- *$80,000 in 401(k)*
- *$5,000 in cash*
- *$10,000 credit card debt*

By reallocating some of her assets, Patricia had added another $150 to her monthly income, which she automatically directed to her daughter's college fund. And because it was a real estate property, she had the advantages of depreciation. She also added another entity to her expense management. Now that she was doing the right thing at the right time, Patricia's Cash Machine provided her with the entities that would allow her to forecast her spending. These building blocks involved the use of tax strategies that allowed Patricia to retain more of her earnings and put those additional monies toward her Wealth Accounts and Debt Management.

	PERSONAL	LLC WEB DESIGN	LLC REAL ESTATE	TOTAL
REVENUE				
EXPENDITURES				
ASSETS				
LIABILITIES				

As Patricia paid into her *Wealth Account* she also began to focus on Debt Management through the Five-Step *Debt Elimination* plan. In six months she paid $3,000 toward her debt, the same amount she'd paid over six months into each of her two Wealth Accounts. Because her Web design business was doing so well, and Patricia was managing her expenses much better, she was able to substantially lower her $10,000 credit card debt in 12 months and eliminate it altogether in two years.

As soon as Patricia decided to stop complaining about having to build a Web design business, I knew that she was committed to *Leadership* and leading her wealth. In order to succeed, Patricia needed to maintain her lifestyle and commit to her Cash Machine. This would mean *Conditioning* herself to take control of her relationship to money. She would also make this shift in mindset easier for her daughter by including her in the business. Patricia would then need *Teamwork* to build a strong team to reach her Asset and Cash Machine goals. Clearly communicating her vision and sharing her passion with others would get them on board.

A Virtual MBA, Only Better

When Patricia was ready to venture beyond her Web design company to establish the summer camp, it was as if she had an MBA's worth of life experience. Patricia was miles ahead of where she'd been when she first wanted to pursue this option, and as a result, she was more efficient and effective in realizing her vision. Though the company was in essence a nonprofit, Patricia structured it as a true business, drawing up a polished and presentable business directive to secure educational grants and personal contributions, creating high-quality marketing materials to attract campers and support fundraising efforts, selecting an advisory board, and hiring first-rate staff. Only recently a project manager making $45,000 a year, Patricia began to live in a world where she was doing what she wanted to do, resources were plentiful, her leadership was recognized and admired, and her vision had become reality.

Making it is one thing, keeping it is another . . .

6

ENTITIES
Getting Your House in Order

I met Kerry Kingsley a few years before I'd worked with the television producer and the Leonard family. Kerry was 63, single, and lived in Scottsdale, Arizona; her kids were grown and on their own. When we met, Kerry had made a lot of money with her own businesses, but she didn't have any personal wealth. And she needed it: her mother was ailing and needed care, and although Kerry loved her work, circumstances demanded that she work less.

Plan for Abundance

When we met, Kerry had already started investing in real estate, owned two businesses—an executive search firm and a staffing company—and had, in fact, created entities for these investments in the form of three S corporations. But, as you'll see in the explanation of S corporations below, the income and expenses from Kerry's businesses were flowing through to her personal income tax return each year. By not properly structuring her businesses, Kerry was setting herself up for a heavy tax burden.

Kerry needed to implement entity structuring that would make better use of tax strategies. When Kerry described her business situation and entity structure, I said, "You need more people and more help." As you'll see, this example provides an interesting sample sequence of building blocks and underscores the importance of Leadership and Teamwork in the building blocks of the Wealth Cycle.

We drew out the schematic for her Gap Analysis, and Kerry easily answered the eight questions in fewer than eight minutes.

Question 1: What Is Your Monthly Income?

Gap Analysis	Financial Baseline	Entities

"$15,000 a month."

ONE-YEAR FREEDOM DAY GOALS	
REVENUE	ASSETS
FINANCIAL BASELINE	
PRETAX INCOME: $15,000/month	ASSETS:
EXPENDITURES:	LIABILITIES:
SKILL SET:	
• $9,000/month from the executive search firm • $6,000/month from the staffing company	

Question 2: What Are Your Monthly Expenditures?

"I spend about $5,000 each month," she said. "After taxes, that's about all I have left." We had to get Kerry to a place where she could retain much more of what she was earning.

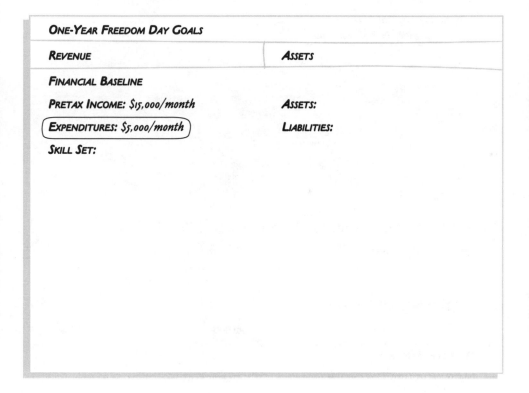

ONE-YEAR FREEDOM DAY GOALS

REVENUE	ASSETS
FINANCIAL BASELINE	
PRETAX INCOME: $15,000/month	ASSETS:
EXPENDITURES: $5,000/month	LIABILITIES:
SKILL SET:	

Question 3: What Assets Do You Have?

"I have about $1 million in properties, and I have $500,000 of equity in my house."

ONE-YEAR FREEDOM DAY GOALS

REVENUE	*ASSETS*
FINANCIAL BASELINE	
PRETAX INCOME: $15,000/month	*ASSETS: $1,500,000*
EXPENDITURES: $5,000/month	*LIABILITIES:*
SKILL SET:	

- *$1,000,000 invested in real estate*
- *$500,000 equity in her own home*

Question 4: What Are Your Liabilities?

"A $200,000 mortgage on the house and $700,000 in debt on the properties I own."

ONE-YEAR FREEDOM DAY GOALS

REVENUE	*ASSETS*
FINANCIAL BASELINE	
PRETAX INCOME: $15,000/month	*ASSETS: $1,500,000*
EXPENDITURES: $5,000/month	*LIABILITIES: $900,000*
SKILL SET:	

- *$1,000,000 invested in real estate*
- *$500,000 equity in her own home*
- *$200,000 mortgage on her house*
- *$700,000 mortgage against real estate*

Question 5: What Else?

"I have $30,000 in a SEP-IRA, and, well, if you mean like in the bank, I have $125,000 in cash."

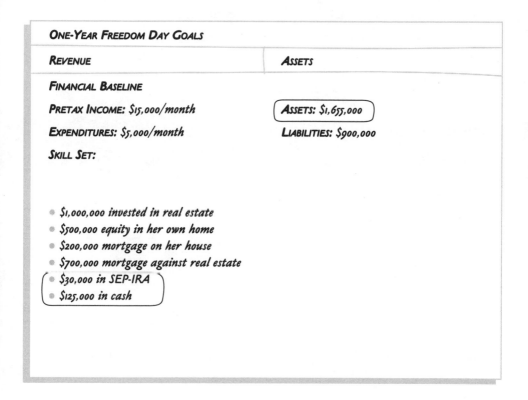

ONE-YEAR FREEDOM DAY GOALS

REVENUE	**ASSETS**
FINANCIAL BASELINE	
PRETAX INCOME: *$15,000/month*	**ASSETS: $1,655,000**
EXPENDITURES: *$5,000/month*	**LIABILITIES:** *$900,000*
SKILL SET:	

- *$1,000,000 invested in real estate*
- *$500,000 equity in her own home*
- *$200,000 mortgage on her house*
- *$700,000 mortgage against real estate*
- *$30,000 in SEP-IRA*
- *$125,000 in cash*

Question 6: What Do You Want?

"I think I'd like three times the amount of monthly cash flow I have now. I'd like to keep more of it, and develop my business without working more."

ONE-YEAR FREEDOM DAY GOALS
- *Create $45,000/month cash flow*
- *Build the business, work less*
- *Ensure care for her mother*
- *Keep more money through entity structuring*

REVENUE	ASSETS

FINANCIAL BASELINE

PRETAX INCOME: *$15,000/month*

EXPENDITURES: *$5,000/month*

SKILL SET:

ASSETS: *$1,655,000*

LIABILITIES: *$900,000*

Question 7: What Skills Do You Use to Make Money?

Gap Analysis   Cash Machine

"I'm a human resources professional. I have a search firm. I'm very good at communicating and networking and taking care of people," she said. "That's what I do, take care of people. I think I do that too much, actually."

ONE-YEAR FREEDOM DAY GOALS
- *Create $45,000/month cash flow*
- *Build the business, work less*
- *Ensure care for her mother*
- *Keep more money through entity structuring*

REVENUE	**ASSETS**

FINANCIAL BASELINE

PRETAX INCOME: *$15,000/month*   **ASSETS:** *$1,655,000*

EXPENDITURES: *$5,000/month*   **LIABILITIES:** *$900,000*

SKILL SET: *Human resource management, communication, networking*

Question 8: Are You Willing to Create and Execute the Wealth Cycle Process?

Gap Analysis   Leadership

"Oh, yes," she said. "Absolutely."

"Yes is the right answer," I said.

From the eight questions in eight minutes, Kerry's Gap Analysis looked like this:

ONE-YEAR FREEDOM DAY GOALS
- *Create a $45,000/month cash flow*
- *Build the business but work less*
- *Ensure care for her mother*
- *Keep more money through entity structuring*

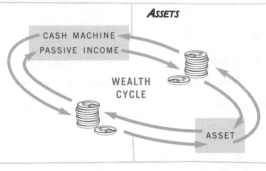

REVENUE

ASSETS

CASH MACHINE
PASSIVE INCOME

WEALTH
CYCLE

ASSET

FINANCIAL BASELINE

PRETAX INCOME: $15,000/month   *ASSETS: $1,655,000*

EXPENDITURES: $5,000/month   *LIABILITIES: $900,000*

SKILL SET: Human resource management, communication, networking

- *$1,000,000 invested in real estate*
- *$500,000 equity in her own home*
- *$200,000 mortgage on her house*
- *$700,000 mortgage against real estate*
- *$30,000 in SEP IRA*
- *$125,000 in cash*

I saw Kerry's sequence immediately. We needed to fix her entities structure and then make sure that her Cash Machine was making enough money to feed her Wealth Cycle.

Gap Analysis ➤ Financial Baseline ➤ Freedom Day

Entities ➤ Forecasting ➤ Cash Machine ➤

Wealth Account ➤ Assets ➤ Debt Management

Leadership + Conditioning + Teamwork

Kerry Kingsley's Wealth Plan

With the essential information laid out in front of us, we were ready to engage Kerry's Wealth Cycle Process. The *Gap Analysis* made clear that Kerry was very good at making money, but she just wasn't great at keeping it. What jumped out at me from Kerry's *Financial Baseline* was the amount of income she had in relation to her assets. She needed a better way to make money and structure her assets.

In terms of identifying a *Freedom Day*, Kerry's goal was to triple her income, which meant $45,000 each month in cash flow. By restructuring her entities and shoring up her Cash Machine, Kerry could keep more of her revenue, build her business, and ensure her mother's care.

Kerry's *Entities* needed immediate attention. Although Kerry was smart enough to put her real estate holdings in a corporate structure, she'd chosen the wrong entities. While one S corporation is a good idea for Kerry's business, she needed an LLC for her real estate to protect her against liability. Additionally, because Kerry made so much money from her Cash Machine, she was getting clobbered every year on the taxes that passed through the S corporations at the end of each year. A good accountant would have explained the importance of creating a C corporation for one of her companies, for example, the search firm, and maintaining an S corporation for the other, the staffing firm.

In a C corporation (a corporation that has elected to be taxed under Subchapter C of the Internal Revenue Code), the company's income and expenses stick with the company. Kerry would earn money either from a salary paid by the company or from a dividend or distribution that the company paid to her. Thus Kerry's search firm, which has assets and employees, could engage in certain tax strategies not available to an S corporation. The C corporation could also market, manage, and provide the services, operations, and distribution of products of her S corporation. The fees the C corporation would charge would then come out of the S corporation's pretax dollars. The C corporation would not only have its own expenses to deduct but could end its fiscal year at any time during the year so as to defer some of those tax obligations.

In addition, to increase the revenue generated from her Cash Machine, Kerry was considering adding some product (for example, human resources training manuals) to her revenue model. The C corporation could also manage the manufacturing, marketing, operations, fulfillment, and administration of these products.

The Importance of Entities

If you want to be a millionaire, you need to act like one. Most wealthy people I know have multiple corporations and trusts, as well as charities: for example, the Bill and Melinda Gates Foundation. The purpose of these entities is to

1. Maximize tax strategies
2. Create liability protection
3. Ensure asset protection
4. Keep wealth accelerating through multiple streams of revenue
5. Optimize opportunities

It is imperative that you understand the available legal entities and their tax implications. By some estimates there are 60,000 pages in the tax code, yet most CPAs in this country use only 50 to 100 of them in serving their clients. That's probably why on April 15, 2005, Americans overpaid billions in taxes. It is your obligation to find a

CPA or financial planner who knows how to support your plan. They exist—just ask around. Your mentors are a terrific source for recommendations, and there are several other resources available. If you can't find them, check the Resources section at the back of this book. A good CPA will prove to be one of the most important members of your wealth-building, and more important, your wealth-sustaining, team.

As we move forward to eliminate debt and build your Wealth Cycle, we are going to structure your life as if you are already wealthy. We are creating the structure into which you will welcome your wealth. Money will not come to chaos, so we need to build a house to welcome and protect your wealth. There are several advantages to keeping your money in entities rather than in your personal bank account. The biggest is that you secure proper asset protection and minimize your risk, giving yourself every opportunity to increase and sustain the asset base and, as a result, your wealth. At the very least, you will protect your assets—the businesses, real estate, intellectual property, and any proprietary technology, processes, services, or products you develop. In addition, you protect yourself from personal liability, create privacy for your wealth, separate your wealth from the commotion of your personal world, and maximize tax strategies within the legal rights prescribed in the tax code.

There are two primary tax structures under U.S. law: one for employees and one for corporations. As you know, employees are taxed on what they earn, and usually these taxes are withheld from employees' paychecks. Corporations, on the other hand, manage their own taxes; this management includes deducting appropriate business expenses. In the United States, there are a number of legal structures that may be used by individuals to hold and protect wealth. These are separate and distinct from the taxpayers who own them, each with its own Employer Identification Number (EIN) unrelated to any individual's Social Security number. The legal protections, tax implications, and personal responsibilities and liabilities differ for each of these entities. How a person structures his or her investments and uses these vehicles can have enormous tax and legal implications.

The following is a brief explanation of entities that are commonly used by the wealthy, and which, with advice from a lawyer or accountant, you must consider if you are going to build a Wealth Cycle. Because each state annually changes the regulations for entity structures, the continued advice of an attorney or a CPA is important in order to stay current. Again, take the time to find a good lawyer and a good accountant, because these people will be an integral factor in your ability to succeed. The examples below are available in the United States, and equivalents exist and operate similarly in many countries around the world.

C Corporations

This is a standard business corporation and represents the most typical structure for a for-profit entity that pays taxes on the income it generates. The C refers to Subchapter C of the IRS code, under which this corporation is taxed. When you form a C corporation, you've created a legal entity separate from yourself, and shareholders have no personal liability for the corporation's debts or actions. It acts on its own authority, it files its own taxes, and it can have an unlimited number of shareholders, which in and of themselves may be legal entities.

C corporations own their own assets, incur their own liabilities, and can provide goods or service. They meet the requirements for about 300 deductible expenses. The fiscal year is flexible in that it can end at any time—typically at the end of the regular calendar year (December 31), or after any quarter (March 31, June 30, or September 30), or for that matter at any time. These corporations are taxed on their operating income, and all dividends are considered taxable income, which means, in effect, that shareholders of a C corporation will be double-taxed, with the government first taking a bite out of the corporation's operating income and then, depending on the tax law at the time, taking another out of the dividends paid to the business owners. On the advantage side, though, C corporations enjoy a low tax rate on the first $50,000 the company earns.

Creating a C corporation and then hiring that corporation to manage other entities, as I suggested Kerry Kingsley do, can in some cases create opportunities to reallocate cash flow over different fiscal years and also allow various tax deductions.

S Corporations

These are typically smaller corporations, with no more than 75 owners, but like the C corporations, they are legal entities authorized by state law that protect shareholders from legal liability. They are sometimes called Subchapter S, because they are taxed under Subchapter S of the IRS code. These corporations pay no income tax. All profits and losses pass straight through to the shareholders, who then assume liability for the taxes; however, the shareholders are not doubly taxed, as they are in a C corporation. This makes them more like a partnership. S corporations meet the requirements for approximately 150 allowable expense deductions and can be used as part of a multicorporation strategy. They are also useful for newer businesses in that S corporations can flow their losses through to the individual, thus reducing their personal income. Congress and the IRS established this chapter of the tax code to encourage start-up businesses by giving the owners this use of losses against other income. If and when the company starts to earn more income, the owners can easily switch the tax status from Subchapter S to Subchapter C.

Limited Partnership

A limited partnership is not a corporation but a business organization with one or more general partners and one or more limited partners. A limited partnership is an entity created according to state law and registered and approved by the secretary of the state where it is created. A limited partnership is to be distinguished from a general partnership, which is not typically a separate tax entity but a pass-through entity, meaning that business income passes through to the partners, who then report their share of profits or losses on their individual returns. In a limited partnership, the general partners are the active investors who manage the business and are liable for all its financial debts and legal obligations. No matter how much or little of the assets they own, they are responsible for 100 percent of them. The limited partners are passive investors who share in the cash flow, but do not share in the authority of the business; nor are they exposed to any liability other than the personal risk of their investment. Often the general partner is a corporation; the corporation is responsible for all financial and legal liability, but the people who own the shares of that corporation are not. The assets of the general partner are always at risk. All partners contribute to finance the business, either through cash or something of comparable value, such as property or sweat equity. I find that limited partnerships are useful when the parties involved do not wish to be on equal footing and one party would like to remain passive and unaccountable, while others manage the partnership's activities.

Family Limited Partnerships

Family Limited Partnerships (FLPs) are limited partnerships where the majority of the partners are family members. Pending legislation regarding estate and death taxes, these are powerful entities for protecting a family's assets and as an estate-planning tool.

An FLP's structure is the same as a limited partnership, except that the parents or grandparents put their assets into the partnership, act as the general partner, and gift their limited partner interests to their children or grandchildren. In other words, the parents give up their assets but maintain their control. Although income tax liability passes through to partners automatically, cash is distributed only at the discretion of the general partners. In an FLP, children under 14 pay no taxes, but as soon as they turn 14 they take on the burden represented by their proportional ownership of the FLP.

Limited Liability Company

The Limited Liability Company (LLC) is neither a partnership nor a corporation. It is a particular type of organization that many find combines the best of both corporations and partnerships. As a separate entity for liability protection, it has the corporate advantage of limited liability. LLC participants are protected from personal liability for LLC debts, except to the extent of their investment in the LLC. The participants of the LLC also receive the partnership-like advantage of pass-through taxation, unless they elect to be taxed as a C corporation. LLC participants are called members, and though a managing member makes the active business decisions, all the LLC's members are treated equally or as agreed upon in their articles of organization or the operating agreement. An LLC is almost identical from both a tax and liability perspective to an S corporation, but the annual reporting requirements and other more flexible tax treatments make them the most popular of entity structures today, particularly for real estate investing.

Trusts

A trust is a legal structure that is used to hold legal title to property for the benefit of one or more persons. There are usually three parties to a trust: (1) the trust creator or grantor, who creates the trust; (2) the trustee, the person or institution holding legal title to the property; and (3) the beneficiary or beneficiaries who are intended to benefit from the trust. The trust serves as a separate entity, used for estate planning and sometimes for asset protection purposes. Typically a trust is outside the reach of creditors and inaccessible as a means of satisfying other debt obligations, but only if it is irrevocable, that is, if it cannot be changed by the grantor, which is not always the case. For example, a family living trust is a revocable trust that allows the assets to avoid going through probate but provides no liability protection. As a result, if you have a living trust and want asset protection, you may need other constructs or entities to protect you from liability. The trust is also outside the reach of the beneficiaries themselves, until a designated date. Trusts can also be used in certain cases to pass a certain amount of property along tax-free.

I always recommend that a trust be the umbrella of your entire organization and all your entities, so that your trust, and not you, is named as a participant in each of your businesses. From now on it's not about you making money; it's about your company making money. Any of these entities may serve your purposes, and it is important to recognize the benefits and limitations of each one. For example, the entities that allow taxes to pass through, such as the S corporation, the LLC, and the trusts, also provide business continuity after you die. I recommend that you consider several legal entities as part of your wealth structure, each serving as a vehicle for like-type assets. It is important to engage a qualified attorney on your team and follow his or her advice as you lead your wealth creation.

Maximizing Tax Strategies

In my experience, most business owners and investors don't make proper use of legitimate business deductions. They pay too many deductible business expenses from their personal funds. This failure frequently costs them substantial amounts of money that could be invested in their business or other wealth-generating assets. The following list identifies some of the typical business expenses that you can deduct to minimize your tax burden. You must have a legal business structure in place in order to take advantage of these deductions. Also, each entity has its own guidelines and legal specifications that determine what can be deducted and for how much. Possible business deductions include

- Utilities
- Computer equipment
- Rent for office or home office deduction
- Phone
- Office supplies
- Employee salaries and bonuses
- Fees for legal, accounting, bookkeeping, coaching, mentoring, and contractors
- Education
- Internet
- Web sites
- Marketing
- Entertainment
- Meals
- Travel
- Car, gas, and insurance
- Corporate housing
- Gifts

No matter what your situation or strategy, proper documentation and an understanding of your financial situation are essential to maximizing your wealth building. This entails maintaining precise accounting records. If you wish to deduct the cost of an item from your taxes, you must be able to justify the deduction by producing the exact cost of the item, the date of the purchase, a description of the purchase, and the business purpose of the purchase. This is where the use of a debit card that itemizes spending or a credit card and statement, if you immediately pay off the balance of the credit card, come in handy. There are some stores I shop where I have to go through the checkout line three times, each with a different credit card, just to keep track.

Again, through mentors and other experts you trust, find a great financial advisor, CPA, or tax strategist to assist you with this process. Though you must lead your team by keeping track of your records, as well as highlighting key pieces you think might be helpful, there is no need for you to study all the intricacies of entity structuring. There are professionals you can turn to so that you can spend your time generating more wealth. Unfortunately, there are plenty of advisors and consultants out there who just don't know as much as other advisors and consultants. With the help of trusted associates and mentors you can find the best professionals available for you and your business. These entities, the creation of which is an ongoing process, provide the structure into which your money can flow. It's important to understand exactly how to manage them through forecasting.

Back to Kerry's Wealth Plan

Given that Kerry has made a lot of money and retained little of it, *Forecasting* would be an important building block in her Wealth

Cycle. My team and I advised Kerry to keep just one of her three S corporations, park another for later use, and get rid of the third. Then we arranged for her to create an LLC for her real estate and a C corporation for her executive search firm. After completing the forecasting step, Kerry's expense management plan looked like this:

	PERSONAL	S CORP STAFFING	LLC REAL ESTATE	C CORP SEARCH FIRM	TOTAL
REVENUE					
EXPENDITURES					
ASSETS					
LIABILITIES					

Though Kerry's business was doing well, we both thought, as a *Cash Machine*, it could be improved. She had created some products to sell along with her services, but it wasn't generating the cash she'd hoped. We put a marketing plan in place and also bundled some of the products with her services to generate interest. Kerry redid her business directive and focused on her marketing and distribution. Additionally, she set up another business just for the marketing of her product, to help her better manage her expenses and keep the product and service expenses from mingling. The acceleration of her marketing and sales efforts, within five months, tripled her business, from $15,000 to $45,000.

Right after Kerry fired her CPA and hired a new one, we set up a personal *Wealth Account* and several holding accounts in each of her entities. She was going to gear up her investment in *Assets* and needed to create her own bank in order to keep up with herself. In terms of assets, Kerry had a total of $1,655,000, which consisted of

- $1,000,000 invested in real estate
- $500,000 equity in her own home
- $30,000 in a SEP
- $125,000 in cash

Plus Kerry was willing to

1. Take $200,000 of the equity out of her house
2. Take $100,000 of equity from her other real estate holdings through a refinancing
3. Shift the $30,000 from her IRAs into a true self-directed IRA
4. Move $100,000 of her cash to a better income-producing asset

All this allowed for a total of $430,000 to be directly allocated into a diverse range of unconventional and aggressive income generating assets.

Because Kerry was already so heavily invested in real estate, she wanted to diversify her assets a bit. She had a few field partners who were starting new businesses, both of which promised immediate cash flow, potential appreciation, and depreciation. Since Kerry had a net worth that gave her accredited status with the IRS and the SEC, I was supportive of her aggressive approach.

Kerry would receive $4,000 a month in passive income; $2,000 a month of this sum would be used to hire additional care for her mother. Kerry's efforts to increase her Cash Machine would now be supplemented without her having to lift a finger. In terms of *Debt Management*, Kerry had a low-interest, fixed-rate mortgage that didn't need to go anywhere and her credit cards didn't carry a balance.

Kerry's *Conditioning* was to be a caretaker. She obviously felt responsible for a lot of people, including her ailing mother. If she was to succeed in managing her Cash Machine, Kerry had to let go of her propensity to do everything herself and get some help through *Teamwork*. In establishing a team, your standards should be high. Kerry needed to take a *Leadership* role. It's important to scrutinize the experts to make sure that you choose the best professionals for your specific needs. Kerry had been getting some bad advice on her entity structuring. I've seen too many accountants who are con-

---

ONE-YEAR FREEDOM DAY GOALS
- *Create a $45,000/month cash flow*
- *Build the business but work less*
- *Ensure care for her mother*
- *Keep more money through entity structuring*

REVENUE	**ASSETS**
CASH MACHINE	**SHIFT ASSETS OF $430,000:**
Tripled business cash flow from $15,000/month to $45,000/month	- *$100,000 into a business that promised 24% annual return*
PASSIVE INCOME	- *$50,000 into a business that promised 24% return*
CASH FLOW:	- *$100,000 promissory note at 12%*
$2000/month	- *$180,000 into a land deal*
$1,000/month	
$1,000/month	
APPRECIATION:	
PROJECTED: *$456,000 in two years*	

FINANCIAL BASELINE

PRETAX INCOME: *$15,000/month*   **ASSETS:** *$1,655,000*

EXPENDITURES: *$6,500/month*   **LIABILITIES:** *$900,000*

SKILL SET: *Human resource management, communication, networking*

- *$1,500/month of increased payment from refinancing 300,000 at 6%*

fused about how to properly structure entities, and who, in fact, create more problems than they solve. Additionally, I've seen certified financial planners who can't think beyond their training, or their fees and commissions, to help their clients utilize the optimal investment vehicles and strategies.

One of the biggest problems I see in wealth building is that people tend to hold back and wait until they feel they need expert advice. That is, they wait until they have some wealth to worry about, when really what they should do is the exact opposite. To finish well, you need to start well. The time when you need really superior advice and expert coaching is in the early stages of wealth building. A good team can keep you from making mistakes that cost you time and money while you're in the learning curve. Even if you are just starting out on your journey to wealth, your objective is to build and lead the best team you can, one made up of leading-edge professionals and experts. You do not need to hire them all now, but you can start to identify who you need and how you can connect with them.

Worrying about the Right Things Now

Once Kerry had her entities in place and properly structured, she was able to focus on building her Cash Machine and fueling her Wealth Cycle. Good advice did wonders for her stress level. Getting the entities right was the first challenge. Then the focus was all about staying diligent in leading her expenditures and forecasting strategies.

The right thing at the right time, in the right place . . .

7

FORECASTING
The Right Stuff
in the Right Bucket

In the Wealth Cycle Process, you will deliberately and purposefully plan how you will spend your money. Rather than looking at your current obligations to see how far you can stretch your earnings, Forecasting pushes you away from the constrained world of small expectations into your greater, grander, and very doable vision. In order to forecast, you need to break out your revenues and expenditures into personal and business, perhaps multiple business, categories. The initial effort should be to maximize your tax strategies by creating entities and making sure to deduct all your legitimate business expenses instead of carrying them on the back of your personal accounts. Every time I worked for a company I always had another source of revenue, a Cash Machine, so that I could forecast my legitimate business expenses through an entity and maximize my tax advantages. For example, when I worked at an oil company, I also had personal health and fitness clients and made about $1,000 extra a month to keep my tax strategy going.

The Leaky Bucket

Jim Quinlin was a personal trainer in Topeka, Kansas. He was 25 and single, and he thought his personal training business was doing well, but apparently it wasn't doing well enough, because he could barely pay his rent. In fact he was losing money every month.

"I thought I was so smart," he said. "I set up all these companies to protect myself, you know, because it's a personal fitness company and I don't want liability. But I'm still making no money. I'm running my company as an LLC, and then I also have an S corp and a C corp, but I don't really use them for anything. I don't know why I have them."

Question 1: What Is Your Monthly Income?

"My business grosses $80,000 a year, and I pay myself $625 a week and pay personal income taxes on that."

ONE-YEAR FREEDOM DAY GOALS

REVENUE	ASSETS

FINANCIAL BASELINE

<u>PRETAX INCOME: $2,500/month</u>   ASSETS:

EXPENDITURES: LIABILITIES:

SKILL SET:

- Business Income: $80,000/year
- Entities: C corp, S corp, LLC

Question 2: What Are Your Monthly Expenditures?

"I spend about $3,000 a month," Jim said. "For personal, that's not business stuff."

ONE-YEAR FREEDOM DAY GOALS

REVENUE	ASSETS

FINANCIAL BASELINE

PRETAX INCOME: $2,500/month   ASSETS:

<u>EXPENDITURES: $3,000/month</u>   LIABILITIES:

SKILL SET:

Jim Quinlin's finances were upside down. His expenditures plus his taxes were greater than his income. Jim's company made $80,000 a year, and he was probably paying half of it in taxes because he was not properly using his entities. Once we taught Jim how to forecast, he'd be retaining a lot more of his revenue and quickly get right side up.

Question 3: What Assets Do You Have?

"My business, I guess. Though it's just me and a few weights. I have a whopping $5,000 in the SEP I created and that's it. I rent my apartment."

ONE-YEAR FREEDOM DAY GOALS	
REVENUE	ASSETS
FINANCIAL BASELINE	
PRETAX INCOME: $2,500/month	ASSETS: $5,000
EXPENDITURES: $3,000/month	LIABILITIES:
SKILL SET:	
• $5,000 in SEP-IRA	

Question 4: What Are Your Liabilities?

"I owe some money on my business, about $30,000. For the store-front I've been leasing and for some marketing and equipment, stuff like that."

ONE-YEAR FREEDOM DAY GOALS

REVENUE	ASSETS

FINANCIAL BASELINE

PRETAX INCOME: *$2,500/month*

EXPENDITURES: *$3,000/month*

SKILL SET:

ASSETS: *$5,000*

LIABILITIES: *$30,000*

• *$30,000 bank debt for his business*

Question 5: What Else?

"I seem to always have about $3,000 on my credit card I can't get off of there."

ONE-YEAR FREEDOM DAY GOALS

REVENUE	ASSETS

FINANCIAL BASELINE

PRETAX INCOME: *$2,500/month*

EXPENDITURES: *$3,000/month*

SKILL SET:

ASSETS: *$5,000*

LIABILITIES: *$33,000*

• *$3,000 credit card debt*

Question 6: What Do You Want?

"I think I'd like some money," Jim said. "I'd actually like to touch and see the money I make, you know?" I did know, exactly. "I think I could be making $200,000 in my business, maybe start creating some products to sell, get to where I have $100,000 in new invested assets, and I'd like to have cash flow of about $5,000 a month. That I actually touch. And I'd like to get that debt way down."

ONE-YEAR FREEDOM DAY GOALS
- *$200,000 business*
- *$100,000 invested assets*
- *$5,000/month cash flow*
- *Debt elimination plan*

REVENUE	ASSETS
FINANCIAL BASELINE	
PRETAX INCOME: *$2,500/month*	ASSETS: *$5,000*
EXPENDITURES: *$3,000/month*	LIABILITIES: *$33,000*
SKILL SET:	

Question 7: What Skills Do You Use to Make Money?

Gap Analysis   Cash Machine

"I'm a personal trainer," he said. "I know physiology and nutrition and I have good people skills. And I organize and run my business. Budgeting and stuff. A little marketing. Obviously not enough."

ONE-YEAR FREEDOM DAY GOALS
- *$200,000 business*
- *$100,000 invested assets*
- *$5,000/month cash flow*
- *Debt elimination plan*

REVENUE	**ASSETS**

FINANCIAL BASELINE

PRETAX INCOME: *$2,500/month*   **ASSETS:** *$5,000*

EXPENDITURES: *$3,000/month*   **LIABILITIES:** *$33,000*

(**SKILL SET:** *Fitness, nutrition, relationships*)

Question 8: Are You Willing to Create and Execute the Wealth Cycle Process?

"Yes," Jim said.

From the eight questions in eight minutes, Jim's Gap Analysis looked like this:

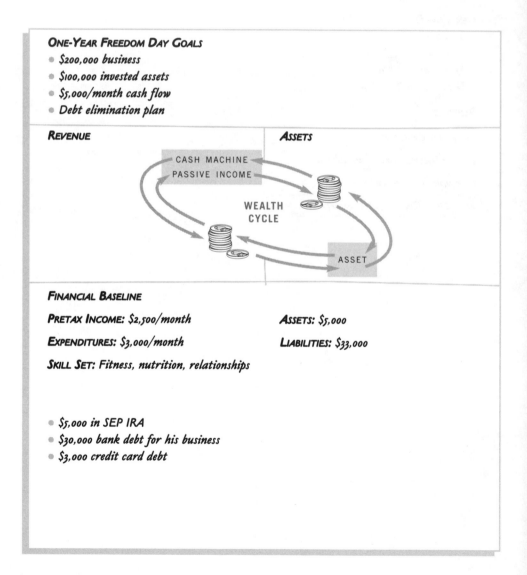

ONE-YEAR FREEDOM DAY GOALS
- *$200,000 business*
- *$100,000 invested assets*
- *$5,000/month cash flow*
- *Debt elimination plan*

REVENUE

ASSETS

CASH MACHINE
PASSIVE INCOME

WEALTH
CYCLE

ASSET

FINANCIAL BASELINE

PRETAX INCOME: $2,500/month

EXPENDITURES: $3,000/month

SKILL SET: Fitness, nutrition, relationships

ASSETS: $5,000

LIABILITIES: $33,000

- *$5,000 in SEP IRA*
- *$30,000 bank debt for his business*
- *$3,000 credit card debt*

Jim needed some help with his sequencing. He was doing some of the right things, only at the wrong time, the most dangerous maneuver in wealth building. He was using the LLC for his business, which meant he was probably paying too much self-employment tax. And he'd not correctly managed his spending forecast. Jim needed some help with expense management and increasing his business revenue.

Gap Analysis ➤ Financial Baseline ➤ Freedom Day

Forecasting ➤ Cash Machine ➤ Debt Management ➤
Wealth Account ➤ Assets ➤ Entities

Conditioning + Teamwork + Leadership

Jim Quinlin's Wealth Plan

According to his *Gap Analysis,* Jim was a victim of taxable money. Though Jim was not paying his taxes with employee status and was in fact paying his taxes as a corporate entity, he was not utilizing the entities correctly, and he still had too much money and liability going into his personal accounts.

Jim needed to increase the money he was making, and keep more of it. The *Financial Baseline* objective would be to better align his entities with his business model so that each represented a bucket into which the proper revenue went in and the proper expenditures came out. His revenue wasn't going into the right buckets, and he was, most likely, paying a bunch of extra tax. But if you don't pattern your money, it gets held up, you won't get taxed right, nor will you grow. Each person has to develop his or her own pattern, but once it's established and you execute within that pattern, you'll own it. And every time you need to accelerate your Wealth Cycle, you'll adjust the pattern.

Jim's business was making enough money for me to think that he could make much more. Plus, he was coming to my team and me for coaching at 25. The guy had ambition and the perspective to know that he needed help to get to where he wanted to go; this would drive Jim toward his *Freedom Day.*

Jim needed to run his personal training business out of his S corporation and make better use of his C corporation. Once we went through the *Forecasting* step, it was clear to me that he needed to create another Cash Machine, such as a network marketing company that sells nutritional supplements, to fuel his personal training business. This would be the C corporation. The C corporation would manage and market that new business, as well as provide services for the S corporation, such as the purchase of equipment and products. Jim would also have to ask a CPA to transition his LLC so it could be used for a planned real estate transaction. Forecasting is about creating a paper trail and keeping it simple. For this, Jim needed a chart of accounts for each of his entities to provide him with the maximum tax strategies and a chart for expense management.

	PERSONAL	S CORP PERSONAL TRAINING	C CORP NETWORK MARKETING COMPANY	LLC FOR FUTURE REAL ESTATE	TOTAL
REVENUE					
EXPENDITURES					
ASSETS					
LIABILITIES					

	PERSONAL	S CORP	C CORP	LLC
REVENUES				
SAVINGS INTEREST				
PERSONAL TRAINING				
TRAINING PRODUCTS				
TRAINING ADMINISTRATIVE				
INVESTMENTS				
GROSS REVENUES				
EXPENDITURES				
WEALTH ACCOUNT				
COST OF GOODS				
STOREFRONT LEASE				
HOME OFFICE				
HOME ASSOC. FEES				
UTILITIES				
WATER				
SEWAGE				
ELECTRICITY				
AUTO EXPENSES:				
LLC				
LEASE				
INSURANCE				
GAS/PARKING				
PERSONAL				
LEASE				
INSURANCE				
GAS/PARKING				
EDUCATION				
OTHER				
TOTAL EXPENDITURES	$	$	$	

These examples reflect how the entities you create play a vital and interdependent role in your capacity to manage your expenditures and focus on your wealth building. In my experience, this step is where the majority of people need the most support. But once they've mastered it, it's the area they find easiest to maintain. Once again, an experienced wealth team will help you do this correctly.

Conscious Spending

Forecasting is done every month in order to chart exactly how much you're spending and what you're spending it on. Examples include housing, education, clothes, food, and debt payments. This will help you see exactly where your money is going. A software program is the best way to track spending. The optimal approach to listing your monthly spending is to remember "If in doubt, don't leave it out." Points are earned for most improved, so make it as bad as you can, be brutally honest and inclusive.

	MONTHLY AMOUNT	
SPENDING CATEGORY	CURRENT	FORECASTED
WEALTH ACCOUNT PRIORITY PAYMENTS		
PERSONAL		
S CORP, HOLDING ACCOUNT		
C CORP, HOLDING ACCOUNT		
LLC, HOLDING ACCOUNT		
DEBT JUMP-START ALLOCATION		
EMERGENCY FUND (3 MONTHS' INCOME IN SAVINGS)		
COST OF GOODS		

CREDIT CARD PAYMENTS		
NO. 1		
NO. 2		
COLLEGE FUND		
TAXES		
RENT		
DAY CARE		
CAR PAYMENT 1		
CAR PAYMENT 2		
UTILITIES		
CABLE		
CELL PHONE		
LOAN		
HEALTH CARE		
FOOD		
GAS		
ENTERTAINMENT		
OTHER		
OTHER		
OTHER		
TOTAL EXPENSE		
TOTAL INCOME		
DIFFERENCE (ADD INTO A WEALTH ACCOUNT OR DEBT JUMP START)		

Now that you have your current spending habits spelled out in front of you, you can rebuild them to work toward achieving your goals. By purposefully forecasting your spending, you will use every single penny that you have to its full advantage. Detail where you must spend money and how much you have to spend in each instance. This will consist of the items you need to live. Within this list of essentials, you want to see which numbers are shouting out as too big; this might direct you to areas in which you are over-spending. Try to narrow in on old spending habits that don't make sense anymore to see how much money you can free up.

Spending can no longer be an unconscious or thoughtless act fueled by the conditioning of your subconscious self. Now that you've come to see how to have a healthy relationship to money and generate wealth, you need to be thoughtful in your approach to your expenditures. Again, this doesn't mean giving up everything you love. It does mean becoming conscious of some of the over- and underallocations that may have slipped your attention. Then, in the Forecast column, reallocate your money to get where you want to go. Now that you have an understanding of Lifestyle Cycles versus Wealth Cycles, you can make a conscious choice to rescue the money from the depths of poor spending and put it into a Wealth Account as well as toward eliminating debt. I always suggest that people spend with intention, not with emotion. There can't be changes to the plan just because of an "Oh, I like that" reaction. You can have an emotional money pool, but you should limit the amount in that pool. When you truly forecast, you'll want all of your money to be allocated to a spending category. The Difference line item should be zero. If each cent is purposefully spent, you elimi-nate emotional spending and recondition your mindset and your relationship to money.

Forecasting is a strategic and ongoing process that changes as you and your finances grow. Without forecasting, you'll continue to overpay in taxes, spend emotionally, and squander money. This is a vital and important strategic step in creating wealth. The Monthly Amount chart gives you a glimpse of the type of high-end tactics you'll come to understand as you advance in your wealth building. Right now, this probably seems foreign because you really haven't learned it yet, but plodding through it will start conditioning you for your future wealth.

Back to Jim's Wealth Plan

I had more than a few ideas of how Jim could increase his *Cash Machine* to reach his goal of a $200,000-a-year business. He was currently charging $60 an hour per client. To make $80,000 a year meant he was billing just under 30 hours of training each week.

I wasn't convinced that Jim could raise his rates by too much in Topeka, Kansas. But if he could include nutritional consulting in his training, he could probably adjust his rate to $75 an hour. He could also increase his billable hours to 60 a week by hiring another trainer. With these new numbers, Jim's business could gross $216,000 a year. By selling the nutritional products, Jim's revenue would also increase, and his reconstructed spending forecast would allow him to keep more of it. I also suggested that Jim invest in producing training videos and scout Topeka for more corporate accounts.

In terms of *Debt Management*, Jim had two levels of debt to contend with: senior bank debt at 12 percent and credit card debt at 18 percent interest. With his entities properly structured and his Cash Machine ramped up, Jim's company was creating and retaining more money. Jim eliminated his credit card debt through our Five-Step Debt Elimination Plan. Then he went to work on paying off his business loan.

The *Wealth Account* step would be Jim's key to achieving $100,000 in invested assets in one year. In Jim's forecasting, he needed to include a WAPP, for his personal Wealth Account, as well as a WAPP for holding accounts in each of his three companies. And he needed to contribute about $2,100 a month into each of these four accounts. This amplification of his Wealth Accounts would position Jim to build to $100,000 in direct asset allocation within a year.

Jim had $5,000 in *Assets,* which consisted solely of the money in his SEP-IRA. With that he wanted to take the $5,000 out of his SEP and put it into a True Self-Directed IRA. But he did not want to use that money for asset allocation until he was ready to accelerate his Wealth Cycle. Jim decided to wait until he had $6,000 in the holding account of at least one of his businesses and then he would use that money to invest in real estate.

ONE-YEAR FREEDOM DAY GOALS
- *$200,000 business*
- *$100,000 invested assets*
- *$5,000/month cash flow*
- *Debt elimination plan*

REVENUE	**ASSETS**
CASH MACHINE	**FOUR WEALTH ACCOUNTS:**
PERSONAL TRAINING BUSINESS: $216,000 a year	$8,400/month, for $100,000 invested assets
NUTRITIONAL BUSINESS: $75,000 a year	**PENDING:**
TOTAL: $291,000	$6,000 per property, producing $200/month and no appreciation.

FINANCIAL BASELINE

PRETAX INCOME: $2,500/month	**ASSETS:** $5,000
EXPENDITURES: $3,000/month	**LIABILITIES:** $33,000
SKILL SET: Fitness, nutrition, relationships	

In terms of *Entities,* Jim had

- The LLC, the S corp, and the C corp established for his personal business

Jim needed to

- Identify the S corporation for his business (personal training)
- Use the C corporation for his network marketing company, the training videos, and to market his personal training business

He called his CPA and instructed her to

- Transition his personal training to the S corp from the LLC
- Use the LLC for a planned real estate transaction
- Establish a trust to serve as an umbrella for all his companies and holdings.

These modifications to Jim's entities would drastically change his forecasting and help him retain more money. By shifting his *Conditioning,* that is, his thought process on forecasting and entity structuring, Jim Quinlin was able to retain more of his earnings and begin focusing on making more money. And in order to make more money, that is, pump up his Cash Machine, Jim needed to (1) make a commitment to work harder on his business, and (2) maintain his lifestyle and expenditures at their current level.

Kind of a lone ranger out in the Kansas plains, Jim realized he had to focus on *Teamwork* and set about putting a good team in place. His CPA had let him down and he needed to find a better one. In addition, there were hundreds of personal trainers in Topeka who'd already made the mistakes Jim was making. He needed to find a mentor.

Jim had the insight to realize that his finances might not be quite right. By realizing this and taking responsibility to build his wealth, Jim took the *Leadership* initiative on reaching his goals. And one of the most important steps Jim took was establishing his Wealth Account and eliminating his debt. These are the life-changing building blocks at the heart of the Wealth Cycle process.

By cleaning up his house, reorganizing his tax strategies, and pumping up his Cash Machine, Jim engaged and accelerated his Wealth Cycle. The leaky bucket is a common problem in wealth building and easily fixed with the proper use of entities and forecasting. The improvement of these building blocks also helped Jim to amplify his Wealth Accounts, a huge boost to any Wealth Cycle.

To thine own assets be true . . .

8

WAPP
It's All about Me

There's no getting around the fact that most of us grew up thinking that we should operate as follows: make money, spend money. That is not the way to do it. You should not buy a lifestyle. You buy cash flow–producing assets and then you get a lifestyle. That's the proper sequencing.

Big Leased Lifestyle

John and Jean Jones, both in their late fifties, from Cincinnati, Ohio, had the "make money, spend money" equation down pat. Not to mention that they were psychologically invested in looking pretty and staying poor. We'd break them of this psychology.

Question 1: What Is Your Monthly Income?

"We each make $100,000 a year, so together, it's over $16,000 a month," John said.

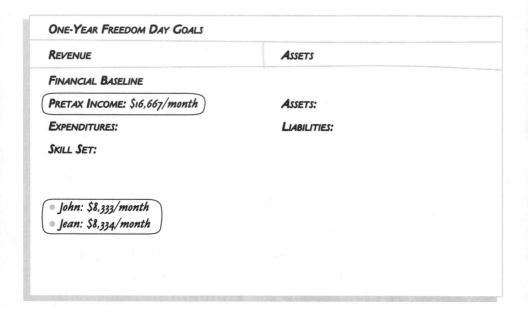

ONE-YEAR FREEDOM DAY GOALS	
REVENUE	ASSETS
FINANCIAL BASELINE	
PRETAX INCOME: $16,667/month	ASSETS:
EXPENDITURES:	LIABILITIES:
SKILL SET:	
John: $8,333/month Jean: $8,334/month	

Question 2: What Are Your Monthly Expenditures?

Jean looked at John embarrassed, but gave him a little nudge with her elbow to answer. "A lot," John said. "We have three nice cars we lease, and we pay a monthly financing fee on our motorboat at our lake house."

"We also have season tickets to the Reds baseball team that we don't ever use," Jean said.

John said, "We could go on fewer vacations."

"No, we can't," she said. "But we certainly don't need to own the entire Sharper Image catalogue." She turned to me. "We have every new gadget ever invented."

Thinking she might let some of those gadgets fly at John, I waved my hands. "What are your monthly expenditures?"

"All that we make after taxes, for sure, plus we charge a lot, it's $10,000 a month, easily," Jean said.

ONE-YEAR FREEDOM DAY GOALS

REVENUE	*ASSETS*
FINANCIAL BASELINE	
PRETAX INCOME: $16,667/month	*ASSETS:*
EXPENDITURES: $10,000/month	*LIABILITIES:*
SKILL SET:	

Question 3: What Assets Do You Have?

"We have our four-bedroom house in an affluent suburb of Cincinnati, and we have probably $200,000 equity built up in that. And our lake house has about $100,000 in equity now," Jean said. "We'd have a lot more if we hadn't pulled some of the equity to buy the boat. And the SUV to pull it, and . . ."

"I'm not sure that's the point, Jean," John said.

"Ah, in your case," I said, "it's exactly the point."

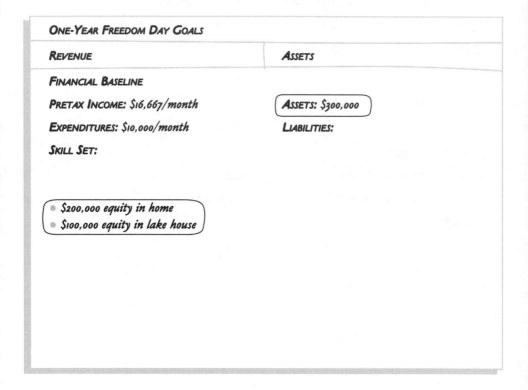

ONE-YEAR FREEDOM DAY GOALS

REVENUE	*ASSETS*
FINANCIAL BASELINE	
PRETAX INCOME: $16,667/month	*ASSETS: $300,000*
EXPENDITURES: $10,000/month	*LIABILITIES:*
SKILL SET:	

- *$200,000 equity in home*
- *$100,000 equity in lake house*

Question 4: What Are Your Liabilities?

Gap Analysis | Financial Baseline | Debt Management

"Him," Jean said.

To his credit, John smiled. "Our liabilities seem endless," John said.

"We have a $600,000 mortgage still on our house, and we have a $200,000 mortgage on our lake house," Jean said.

ONE-YEAR FREEDOM DAY GOALS

REVENUE	ASSETS

FINANCIAL BASELINE

PRETAX INCOME: *$16,667/month*   ASSETS: *$300,000*

EXPENDITURES: *$10,000/month*   LIABILITIES: *$800,000*

SKILL SET:

- *$600,000 mortgage on their home*
- *$200,000 mortgage on their lake home*

Question 5: What Else?

"We have our IRAs," John said. "There's $200,000 there from our jobs. And we have six investment properties that we own personally that we bought down near a resort in Kentucky. They're appreciating; we got 'em for $1 million five years ago, about $167,000 each, and they're each worth $250,000 now. That's $1.5 million now."

"We get monthly income on them too," Jean said.

"But we pay more than that on our mortgage and taxes, so I guess you'd say we're underwater on that?" John said.

"I would. But the other bonus is that you're not getting the full depreciation benefit a professional real estate investor would get because you still have your job."

John cocked his head, not happy.

"Oh, we have $12,000 in credit card debt," Jean said. "Did you mean that too?"

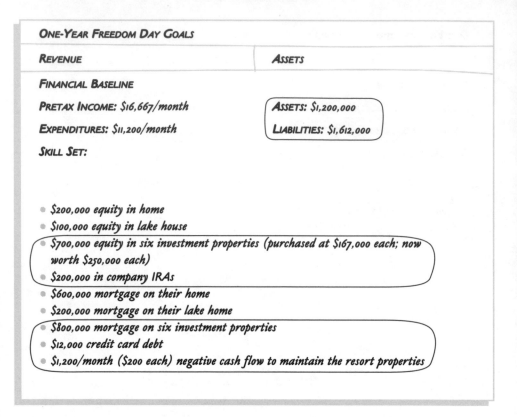

ONE-YEAR FREEDOM DAY GOALS

REVENUE	ASSETS

FINANCIAL BASELINE

PRETAX INCOME: $16,667/month

EXPENDITURES: $11,200/month

ASSETS: $1,200,000

LIABILITIES: $1,612,000

SKILL SET:

- $200,000 equity in home
- $100,000 equity in lake house
- $700,000 equity in six investment properties (purchased at $167,000 each; now worth $250,000 each)
- $200,000 in company IRAs
- $600,000 mortgage on their home
- $200,000 mortgage on their lake home
- $800,000 mortgage on six investment properties
- $12,000 credit card debt
- $1,200/month ($200 each) negative cash flow to maintain the resort properties

Question 6: What Do You Want?

Gap Analysis   Freedom Day

"We'd like a path out of this trap," Jean said.

"No debt," John said

"Assets that perform," Jean said.

"I'd like not to work," John said.

"Me too."

I knew that just getting them balanced would be a challenge. These people were huge retail therapy addicts. Their behavior was so debilitating given their goals; we just had to get them going in the right direction.

ONE-YEAR FREEDOM DAY GOALS
- Reduce debt in an aggressive debt elimination plan
- Shift from draining assets to performing assets
- Establish a business

REVENUE	ASSETS

FINANCIAL BASELINE

PRETAX INCOME: $16,667/month

EXPENDITURES: $11,200/month

SKILL SET:

ASSETS: $1,200,000

LIABILITIES: $1,612,000

Question 7: What Skills Do You Use to Make Money?

"I don't think we have any skills," Jean laughed. "We both work for a huge transportation company here."

"I'm an operations guy, and Jean does finance for them."

169

ONE-YEAR FREEDOM DAY GOALS
- *Reduce debt in an aggressive debt elimination plan*
- *Shift from draining assets to performing assets*
- *Establish a business*

REVENUE	ASSETS

FINANCIAL BASELINE

PRETAX INCOME: *$16,667/month*

EXPENDITURES: *$11,200/month*

ASSETS: *$1,200,000*

LIABILITIES: *$1,612,000*

(**SKILL SET:** *Operations and finance*)

Question 8: Are You Willing to Create and Execute the Wealth Cycle Process?

Gap Analysis   Leadership

"Yes," Jean said.

"Yes, yes, yes," John said.

"Good," I said. "Yes is the right answer.

From the eight questions in eight minutes, the Jones's Gap Analysis looked like this:

ONE-YEAR FREEDOM DAY GOALS
- *Reduce debt in an aggressive debt elimination plan*
- *Shift from draining assets to performing assets*
- *Establish a business*

REVENUE **ASSETS**

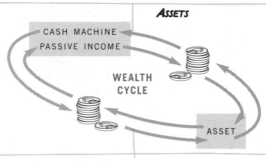

CASH MACHINE
PASSIVE INCOME

WEALTH
CYCLE

ASSET

FINANCIAL BASELINE

PRETAX INCOME: *$16,667/month* **ASSETS:** *$1,200,000*

EXPENDITURES: *$11,200/month* **LIABILITIES:** *$1,612,000*

SKILL SET: *Operations and finance*

- *$200,000 equity in home*
- *$100,000 equity in lake house*
- *$700,000 equity in six investment properties (purchased at $167,000 each, now worth $250,000 each)*
- *$200,000 in company IRAs*
- *$600,000 mortgage on home*
- *$200,000 mortgage on lake home*
- *$800,000 mortgage on the six investment properties*
- *$12,000 credit card debt*
- *$1,200/month negative cash flow to maintain the six investment properties*

At this rate, the Joneses were never going to keep up with themselves. I saw the sequence of their building blocks as follows:

Gap Analysis ➤ Financial Baseline ➤ Freedom Day

Entities ➤ Forecasting ➤ Assets ➤ Wealth Account ➤
Cash Machine ➤ Debt Management

Leadership + Conditioning + Teamwork

Jean and John Jones's Wealth Plan

Based on their *Gap Analysis*, it was clear that Jean and John had a lot of right things going on, but definitely at the wrong times. A little delayed gratification would do them a whole lot of good. The first thing that popped out at us from the analysis was that their six rental properties were part of their personal finances. Their *Financial Baseline* showed that they needed entities. Then we'd reallocate their assets and teach them how to invest money before they spent it.

I'll say it again: money does not come to chaos. Holding six rental properties in a personal checking account causes chaos and works against being able to identify a *Freedom Day*. We immediately took care of the *Entities* building block. This is what I call a "911." We called one of the CPAs we know in our Team-Made Millionaire community and set up two LLCs for the Joneses' properties, establishing a trust to protect all their assets. We also set up an S corporation for the Cash Machine I knew Jean was going to create.

Though a lot of the spending was a lot of spending, through *Forecasting* it was evident that Jean and John also had some legitimate business expenditures that were being paid with posttax dollars. They needed better expense management as well as some conscious spending. For example, they were going to real estate seminars to learn how to better forecast and manage their spending. Given their investments, these seminars were deductible expenditures, but the couple hadn't deducted them. And because Jean and John chose to remain in their salaried jobs while investing in real estate, they were missing out on another huge tax strategy. Depreciation is a valuable accounting tool and depreciation deductions can be used to reduce taxable income. Because they owned property without being professional real estate investors, Jean and John could account for only $25,000 depreciation on the six houses they had in

Kentucky. Income-generating residential property is depreciated over 27½ years, so the Jones could enjoy straight-line depreciation ($1,000,000/27.5) of $36,000 a year on the $1 million cost of their houses. That means they were losing $11,000 a year, $55,000 so far . . . to keep their jobs.

"Which one of you is going to quit your job?" I asked. They both raised their hands.

	PERSONAL	S CORP REAL ESTATE, BUSINESS	LLC PROPERTIES	LLC PROPERTIES	TOTAL
REVENUE					
EXPENDITURES					
ASSETS					
LIABILITIES					

Jean and John had a lot of *Assets*, along with their liabilities. Of their assets, they had $1.2 million that could be invested, including

- $200,000 equity in home
- $100,000 equity in lake house
- $700,000 equity in their six investment properties
- $200,000 in IRAs

They were willing to

- Take the $700,000 of equity out of their investment properties by selling the six properties.

The five years of appreciation of the Kentucky properties was not worth the drain on the Joneses' cash. They could utilize the tax-deferred strategy of a 1031 like-kind exchange that allows a property owner to sell property and reinvest proceeds into ownership of like-kind property and defer the capital gains. I recommended two cash flow–producing commercial properties.

ONE-YEAR FREEDOM DAY GOALS
- *Reduce debt in an aggressive debt elimination plan*
- *Shift from draining assets to performing assets*
- *Establish a business*

REVENUES	ASSETS
PASSIVE INCOME	**SHIFT ASSETS OF $700,000:**
CASH FLOW:	• *$400,000 into a $2 million commercial rental property with 10% return*
$3,333/month	• *$300,000 into a $1.5 million commercial rental property with 15% return*
$3,750/month	

FINANCIAL BASELINE	
PRETAX INCOME: *$16,667/month*	**ASSETS:** *$1,200,000*
EXPENDITURES: *$11,200/month*	**LIABILITIES:** *$1,612,000*
SKILL SET: *Operations and finance*	

Trading up their assets from one cash-draining asset into two cash flow–producing assets had a few benefits for John and Jean Jones: (1) It would create deductions in the form of depreciation of $25,000 a year ($700,000/27.5). (2) It would likely appreciate in value. (3) Instead of being underwater, Jean and John Jones now had just over $7,000 of additional income a month in their first year. This would be a useful infusion into their Wealth Account and in Debt Management.

We had to focus on Jean and John's attitude toward money and create a new habit for them: the *Wealth Account* habit. The thing in between the making of the money and the spending of the money is the outstanding and simple step of paying yourself first. To put their Wealth Cycle in motion, the Joneses needed to set up an interest-bearing Wealth Account, such as brokerage account or a relatively high interest-bearing account, say, 3 percent, from which they could draw to invest in rewarding ventures.

WAPP: The Wealth Account Priority Payment

Pay yourself first is an axiom of the wealthy, and one that should be followed no matter the circumstances. It simply means to take a portion of your earnings and invest it. This payment is a specific amount, paid consistently come rain or shine. Though this is an old concept, it's too often not understood. I've even heard financial advisors confuse this with putting money in savings. I've also heard financial advisors who tell people not to invest any money until they pay off their debt. The concept of pay yourself first is about creating wealth to run circles around your debt, so that you can then spiral up your wealth and easily pay off your debt. In race car jargon, you literally "lap" your debt. Those who do not understand or misunderstand this concept often live in a mindset of fear, the exact scarcity thinking that got many of us to this point.

WAPP is about putting your income into a Wealth Account designated for investing and nothing else. That means you need to set up a Wealth Account and get yourself into the habit of making a Wealth Account Priority Payment every month, preferably an amount automatically withdrawn from your paycheck, to work in assets that generate cash flow. That cash flow will pay off your debt, which will release you from your debt cycle forever.

How the Wealth Account Works

Here's how the Wealth Account works. Once you've established the account, you pay a minimum amount into it on a scheduled basis. This amount—$10, $20, $100, $200, $300, $1,000—and time—weekly or monthly—is at your discretion. I've found that monthly is the easiest. The amount you invest is not nearly as important as starting the process right away. The key to building wealth is to start early and do it often. That means right now. The biggest mistake people make is to wait until they have accumulated a lot of cash or have identified a particular investment. This way of thinking will hold you back from paying yourself first, building the account, and amassing what you need to invest. This step is imperative; it must be done and done now. I'd post this in neon across this page if it would make it any clearer. Every day you do not invest in yourself compounds into days you're not creating wealth. It is very similar to the compound interest you're creating when you sit on debt. As the Wealth Account grows, you will find yourself becoming more aware of investment opportunities and, even better, able to actually consider them.

Though this may seem counterintuitive, priority payment means priority payment, which means you really and truly must pay into your Wealth Account first, before you pay your bills, creditors, or anyone or anything else. Consider it the equivalent of your mortgage, child support, or any other financial obligation. If you can only afford to put in $10 a month, that's all right. You will be amazed at how quickly your wealth will spiral up.

It is helpful to instruct your financial institution to transfer money from your main account to your wealth account via automatic debit system. With automatic transfers, you don't have to worry about forgetting to make deposits into your Wealth Account, you won't have to make the decision every month, and you won't have to deal with deposit slips or postage. You should also set up all your accounts online so that you can review them at any time and at your convenience and make account-to-account transfers. Most financial institutions offer online banking at no additional charge.

Again, as awkward as this may seem, and as uncomfortable as it may be to do, the Wealth Account is the priority payment of the month. Even in the tightest months, pay into your Wealth Account first. This has to be done as regularly as breathing. Even if you are in debt, deposit a portion of your earnings into your Wealth Account now. Remember, the amount you pay each period doesn't matter; the important factor is to form the habit of regularly depositing money into your Wealth Account and building up funds to invest in your future.

I believe you should consider setting aside 10 percent of your income for the Wealth Account. That may seem like a lot, but there are people who belong to certain communities, religions, organizations, and groups that require this type of tithing, and the members manage to accomplish it. The government takes a third of your earnings from your paycheck and you manage to live with that. Add one more bite out of your paycheck and tithe to your own assets. Doing this can become the same habit as not doing this.

Back to the Joneses' Wealth Plan

Though Jean and John Jones had healthy salaries, they were missing out on a good tax strategy by not having their own business. A *Cash Machine* would allow one of them to quit their job, increase their earnings through their own motivation, and take advantage of all the depreciation they could enjoy from their real estate investment properties. Without much background knowledge, John and Jean invested in real estate and doubled their money. I wondered what more they could do if they actually invested some time in learning. Instead of babysitting nonperforming assets, Jean and John could actually nurture some real growth and income. Fortunately, Jean liked buying real estate. She had strong finance skills and I suggested she take some classes to learn more about buying land and properties. I didn't think it was necessary for Jean to get her license, just to advance her skills. The couple was now bringing in just over $7,000 a month in passive income, and John had an income of $8,333 a month. They had about $15,000 a month they could live on without Jean's salary, which had been replaced by the shift in assets and the entity structuring. Given that John knew operations and Jean knew finance, they decided they could create a business advising companies on operational efficiencies, and they were up and running with one client in their first week. Jean quit her job and became a professional real estate investor, and John stayed in his until the Cash Machine ramped up and the Wealth Cycle was in motion and accelerating.

John and Jean needed to change their lifestyle. They had horrible spending habits. Now that they had two Wealth Accounts established, one for their personal account, and one for each of their businesses, they would be making monthly WAPPs. But they needed to focus on *Debt Management* by making equal payments into their debt elimination plan. Since they were still making only what they made before, they needed to manage their lifestyle better. They'd already reduced $1,200 in monthly expenditures by selling the six Kentucky properties, but they'd need to do more. I strongly pushed them to work on their *Forecasting,* which would get them in the habit of conscious spending. While simultaneously building their wealth, John and Jean set up the Five-Step Debt Elimination Plan.

As Jean built up their real estate business, and they both committed to a more managed lifestyle, they were able to commit a large portion of their passive income to pay down their $12,000 of credit card debt. If that debt was going to stay gone, Jean and John needed a lot of coaching on their *Conditioning*. They seemed to have no regard for their money and were partial to immediate gratification.

Talking was not going to do the trick. I knew that once the couple started to take action by shifting assets, establishing their entities, forecasting their spending, building their Cash Machine, and managing their wealth and debt, they would become more aware of the value of a dollar. Nothing conditions the brain to invest like a nice, steady return on investments. As they began to learn more and more about the Wealth Cycle Process, John and Jean switched from retail therapy addicts to asset addicts and focused on the *Teamwork* needed to keep their Wealth Cycle moving. They began to understand the opportunity cost of spending a dollar versus investing it, and their shared objective helped them keep each other accountable with their wealth team.

Soon enough we had the Joneses set up with the appropriate entities. They were forecasting their spending so as to be more conscious spenders and also retain more of their income, and they reallocated many of their assets to create more passive income. They also erased their bad debt. In succeeding in these areas, the Joneses indicated that they had also understood the *Leadership* building block.

Buying the Assets, Living the Life

With a shift in attitude, a shift in assets and an introduction to the very important concept of the WAPP and the Wealth Account, John and Jean Jones were stepping in strong to the Wealth Cycle Process. By focusing on buying assets, instead of buying a lifestyle, John and

Jean were going to have a bigger life than they ever thought possible, and with a lot less stress. The Lifestyle Cycle takes its toll, providing short-term retail therapy for long-term worry. The new mindset of the Joneses had to be keeping up with their wealth and letting the lifestyle follow. Of course, the success of their plan would be contingent on their capacity for debt management.

*Stopping that
downward spiral . . .*

9

DEBT MANAGEMENT
Bad Debt Has Got to Go

A multiple-choice question for you: $8,700 is

   A Just above the U.S. median family income back in 1963
   B Larger than the 2004 per capita income in Oman, Chile, Argentina, Morocco, and over 100 other countries ranked by the World Bank
   C The average spent per pupil in 2003 for a public high school education in Shasta County, California
   D The average personal credit card debt in the United States
   E All of the above

The answer, of course, is E.

That much personal credit card debt is a lot of spending before it's earned and a whole lot of catching up that needs to be done.

The culture has dictated this urgency of consumption, and it's hard not to subscribe to the idea of immediate gratification. But it's undermining our capacity to generate wealth. In order to set the foundation for the Wealth Cycle, we need to eliminate your debt. And we will.

To clarify, we're talking about bad debt only. That means consumer debt, such as high-interest credit card debt that you acquired buying perishable items. We are not talking about good debt, such as any low-interest borrowing you've done to finance a mortgage or student loans, with the interest deductible against your business operations. If you are leveraging debt against an asset, such as your house or your business, then we are going to leave that debt alone. But the bad debt has got to go. And this will be done without declaring bankruptcy, which in almost every single case I have ever seen is an unnecessary step, and without using those debt-aggregating programs, which promise to get you out of debt with one easy monthly payment but end up costing you much more money and time than if you did it yourself. In this process, we will show you how to shrink your bad debt to zero while simultaneously creating cash flow to take care of your expenditures for the rest of your life. Once you realize that cash flow is king, you'll come to understand that if you focus on creating that cash flow, you'll never again have to worry about your expenses overwhelming your income. Unfortunately, Chuck Wallace wasn't there yet.

Lap Your Debt

A 30-year-old math teacher in The Woodlands, Texas, just outside of Houston, with a baby and a wife at home, Chuck came into our Team-Made Millionaire community several years ago. Here's how he responded to the eight questions.

Question 1: What Is Your Monthly Income?

| Gap Analysis | Financial Baseline | Entities |

"I make $3,333 a month."

ONE-YEAR FREEDOM DAY GOALS	
REVENUE	**ASSETS**
FINANCIAL BASELINE	
PRETAX INCOME: *$3,333/month*	ASSETS:
EXPENDITURES:	LIABILITIES:
SKILL SET:	

Question 2: What Are Your Monthly Expenditures?

| Gap Analysis | Financial Baseline | Forecasting |

"With the new baby, I'd say we're easily up to $4,000 a month."

ONE-YEAR FREEDOM DAY GOALS	
REVENUE	**ASSETS**
FINANCIAL BASELINE	
PRETAX INCOME: *$3,333/month*	ASSETS:
EXPENDITURES: *$4,000/month*	LIABILITIES:
SKILL SET:	

Question 3: What Assets Do You Have?

"$5,000 in the teacher's pension fund, $2,000 in the bank. We rent our house."

ONE-YEAR FREEDOM DAY GOALS	
REVENUE	ASSETS
FINANCIAL BASELINE PRETAX INCOME: *$3,333/month* EXPENDITURES: *$4,000/month* SKILL SET: • *$5,000 teacher's pension* • *$2,000 in the bank*	ASSETS: *$7,000* LIABILITIES:

Question 4: What Are Your Liabilities?

"We have $30,000 on credit cards, and with these debt consolidation things I've been doing, I'm still getting pounded on the interest."

ONE-YEAR FREEDOM DAY GOALS	
REVENUE	**ASSETS**
FINANCIAL BASELINE	
PRETAX INCOME: $3,333/month	ASSETS: $7,000
EXPENDITURES: $4,000/month	LIABILITIES: $30,000
SKILL SET:	

• $30,000 in credit cards, consumer debt

Question 5: What Else?

"My wife and I have a total of $20,000 in student loans."

ONE-YEAR FREEDOM DAY GOALS	
REVENUE	**ASSETS**
FINANCIAL BASELINE	
PRETAX INCOME: $3,333/month	ASSETS: $7,000
EXPENDITURES: $4,000/month	LIABILITIES: $50,000
SKILL SET:	

• $20,000 in student loans

Question 6: What Do You Want?

"I don't even know anymore," Chuck said. "I like teaching and all, but I'm just a bit burnt out. And I'm only 30. I guess I'd really like to own and run a bar. I think I'd be very good at it."

"And your numbers?"

"It would be great to have $1,000 a month coming in, free and clear. And less debt. Maybe no debt."

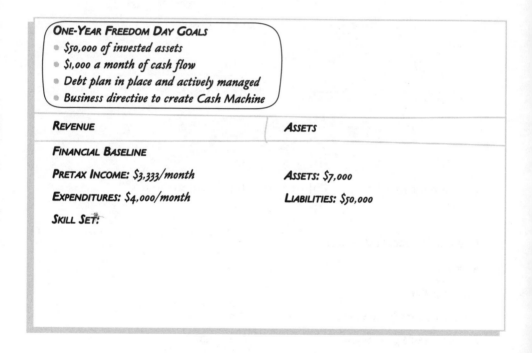

ONE-YEAR FREEDOM DAY GOALS
- *$50,000 of invested assets*
- *$1,000 a month of cash flow*
- *Debt plan in place and actively managed*
- *Business directive to create Cash Machine*

REVENUE	*ASSETS*
FINANCIAL BASELINE	
PRETAX INCOME: $3,333/month	*ASSETS: $7,000*
EXPENDITURES: $4,000/month	*LIABILITIES: $50,000*
SKILL SET:	

Question 7: What Skills Do You Use to Make Money?

"Math, I guess," he said. "But, really, it's about motivating kids."

ONE-YEAR FREEDOM DAY GOALS
- $50,000 of invested assets
- $1,000 a month of cash flow
- Debt plan in place and actively managed
- Business directive to create Cash Machine

REVENUE	ASSETS

FINANCIAL BASELINE

PRETAX INCOME: $3,333/month	ASSETS: $7,000
EXPENDITURES: $4,000/month	LIABILITIES: $50,000

SKILL SET: *Teaching, organization, enthusiasm, leadership, communication*

Question 8: Are You Willing to Create and Execute the Wealth Cycle Process?

Gap Analysis   Leadership

"You bet," he said. "Yes."

From the eight questions in eight minutes, the Gap Analysis looked like this:

ONE-YEAR FREEDOM DAY GOALS
- *$50,000 of invested assets*
- *$1,000/month cash flow*
- *Debt plan in place and actively managed*
- *Business directive to create Cash Machine*

REVENUE   **ASSETS**

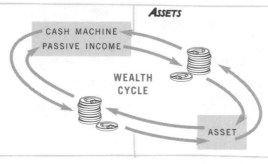

FINANCIAL BASELINE

PRETAX INCOME: *$3,333/month*   **ASSETS:** *$7,000*

EXPENDITURES: *$4,000/month*   **LIABILITIES:** *$50,000*

SKILL SET: *Teaching, organization, enthusiasm, leadership, communication*

- *$5,000 teacher's pension*
- *$2,000 in cash*
- *$30,000 in consumer debt*
- *$20,000 in student loans*

Chuck needed to get out of debt. While many financial experts would put debt elimination at the top of Chuck's to-do list, I knew first things had to come first.

Gap Analysis → Financial Baseline → Freedom Day

Cash Machine → Entities → Forecasting →
Debt Management → Wealth Account → Assets

Conditioning + Teamwork + Leadership

Chuck Wallace's Wealth Plan

In order to bridge the gap, revealed in his *Gap Analysis,* from where he was to where he wanted to be, Chuck Wallace needed to learn how to make and keep more money. His *Financial Baseline* uncovered a low-interest student loan, at 6 percent, but the $30,000 of debt was split between a high-interest credit card and a debt consolidation program. Eliminating the $30,000 would be the priority. But for Chuck to work on bringing down that consumer debt without first working on making money would only frustrate him. It's not easy to pay off $30,000, with interest, when you're only taking home about that much after tax, not to mention all the other expenses Chuck had.

I knew Chuck was capable of turning things around. His goal of $50,000 of invested assets, $1,000 a month of cash flow, managing his debt, and creating a Cash Machine were achievable goals. They were exciting enough to keep him motivated, but not so difficult as to frustrate him in achieving his *Freedom Day.*

I suggested a tutoring business for Chuck's *Cash Machine.*

"Which part of burnt out was I not clear about?" Chuck said.

"I heard you, Chuck," I said. "But this is just to get you to learn to earn. And you don't even need to tutor yourself. You can hire your colleagues. You'll market and manage the business."

Chuck amazed me. He held a party for his colleagues where he solicited tutors, as well as field partners willing to spread the word to students about his services. He ran off flyers and blanketed the county in which he lived. He bought a cell phone and was always available to talk to potential customers. He even put a big poster board on the sides and back of his truck, advertising his business. In the first 120 days of his Wealth Plan, Chuck had 20 students going to two of his colleagues every week. The students each paid $40 an hour and Chuck took half of that.

Given that we needed to get rid of the $30,000 credit card debt to start, and build a wealth account of $50,000, I thought Chuck should try to pay $3,000 a month to his debt elimination plan and $4,000 a month to his wealth account. This would require $86,000 a year. Additionally, Chuck wanted $1,000 a month in cash flow, which made a grand total of $98,000. Chuck's teacher's salary would still cover his expenses, and his entity structuring would help him better manage his expenses to retain more of his income. Given that Chuck had no assets on which he could rely, I thought a goal for the Cash Machine of $100,000 would be challenging but worthwhile. He needed to make $8,333 a month. As Chuck ramped up, he found several more colleagues in a variety of teaching fields looking to be hired and 100 students a week willing to pay them. He was able to increase his hourly fee to $50 an hour, which made his weekly gross $5,000. Chuck took half of this, for a total of $10,000 a month.

For *Entities,* Chuck established an S corporation for his business. Later, we'd create an LLC for his investment opportunities. Chuck had the idea to create tutoring aids and sell these products under a C corporation, so we would establish this as well.

"For someone who is burnt out, you sure have a lot of energy," I said.

"This is fun," he said. "I'm not even sure I want to run a bar anymore."

Numbers being his thing, *Forecasting* was no problem. Chuck set up a very well organized chart of accounts, and because of his new business, he was able to shift some personal expenses into his LLC. This included the part of his rent and utilities that covered his home office, as well as his payments for the company car.

	PERSONAL	S CORP TUTORING	LLC PROPERTIES	TOTAL
REVENUE				
EXPENDITURES				
ASSETS				
LIABILITIES				

And with his *Debt Management* plan in motion, Chuck's looming debt would not be looming for long. The capitalist world is divided into two camps: those who pay interest and those who get paid interest. If you have consumer debt, you're in the wrong camp. Compound interest is a wonderful thing, but only when it's working for you, not against you.

Getting Out of Debt: Bad-Idea Approaches

The following are options for getting out of debt that are less than optimal.

Credit Card Calculus

STRATEGY: To transfer debt from a high-interest-rate credit card to a lower-interest-rate credit card.

COMMON RESULT: After making balance transfers, cardholders usually lose no time in running up their original high-interest cards again. I am amazed by the commitment of time and energy that people put into rotating their credit cards. I can only imagine the success some of the people who do this would have if they put that same creativity and effort into building their passive income. If you are smart enough to play this game, you are smart enough to invest.

Home Equity Loans

STRATEGY: Refinance the home to consolidate debt.

COMMON RESULT: Too many people don't control their spending, borrow more after they refinance, incur more credit card debt and refinance again. Serial refinancers use up all the equity they build and then get boxed out of, or are charged exorbitant interest rates for, additional credit. In many cases, the home that was once a nest egg shuffles off to the brink of foreclosure.

Consolidating Debt

STRATEGY: Allowing a debt-consolidating company to take all of your debt and collapse it into a single, very comfortable monthly payment.

COMMON RESULT: People tend to acquire additional debt after consolidation so that the old debt cycle resurfaces. The reason these payments are so comfortable and low is because they are less than the interest payment. Principal never gets paid down, and the process is endless. Few of these programs are helping you; they're helping themselves by negotiating with, and paying off, your debtors at a discount. Then they pack all your debt in one simple payment that takes twice as long to pay off and ends up costing you more in the long run. In effect, people who lump their debt by refinancing or consolidating are still paying cold hard cash for products and services some 30 years after they were purchased. Those items, most likely, are long gone, but financially not forgotten.

Bankruptcy

STRATEGY: File Chapter 7, personal financial dissolution or liquidation bankruptcy, or Chapter 13, personal financial reorganization or wage-earner bankruptcy. Any expert in the field of personal finance will tell you that this should not even be considered an option.

COMMON RESULT: First, ask anyone who's done it; they probably wish they hadn't. Declaring bankruptcy can seriously disrupt your life, ruin your credit, and taint your reputation, and although you can recover, it will take years. Additionally, it doesn't free you from taxes, which carry substantial penalties and interest. The worst-case scenarios occur when people feel overwhelmed in the moment, because of a series of personal and business malfunctions, declare bankruptcy, only to reemerge two years later with personal and business triumphs and a capacity to get out of the debt. For these people, the ding on the credit excludes them from many lucrative opportunities and wealth building is delayed yet again. If you are contemplating bankruptcy, I can't urge you enough to fully consider all the other options of debt elimination first, study all the facts before filing, and consult a lawyer who specializes in this field—but not one who has any incentive to help you file. You have to live with the consequences for years, and in most cases—in almost all of the cases I have ever seen—bankruptcy is unnecessary. Don't do it.

Credit Repair

STRATEGY: Credit repair companies fix your bad credit.

COMMON RESULT: This can be wonderful, if you deal with a credible repair company. Many legitimate organizations run great programs. But several have surfaced in the past few years that are shady and ruthless. They take your money up front, cost you thousands of dollars, and don't fix your credit. Make sure you get solid references from people you know and trust on any credit repair company, and be wary of online companies that don't have an actual bricks-and-mortar office.

A Five-Step Strategy for Getting Out of Debt

Most people with debt problems are so caught up in their Lifestyle Cycle or their debt juggling that they can't imagine finding a positive solution that will enable them to build wealth. Many would be so grateful to end the pain and panic of debt that they don't think much further than that one issue. Chuck Wallace had made the decision to remove himself emotionally from his debt and the reasons he got into it. For him this became, as it should for you, a pure business venture, a matter of simply applying dollars and cents to abolish debt. Committed to putting the debt plan in place, Chuck had relinquished the idea that he was too far in and only a windfall could save him. Chuck also understood that it takes longer to get out of debt than it does to get into it; but since, as he started to get out of debt, he was also creating wealth, he didn't feel that he was losing any time making himself a millionaire.

I know for a fact that because you want to, you can and will be able to end your role as a debtor and become a lender. By diligently employing basic debt elimination measures, you can get out of the debt cycle within three to seven years and at the same time start to build your Wealth Cycle. It is key to understand that these processes are simultaneous. The following Five-Step Debt Elimination Plan is what we use for all of our clients. If you have debt it will help you begin to get out of that debt, as well as into the habit of the Wealth Account Priority Payment. As you move forward in this process you will note that what makes this different from the other debt elimination processes is that this approach allows you to live a normal life while you eliminate your bad debt. I've actually seen books that make you question why you need to buy any new clothes for a year. I don't know about you, but that doesn't work for me. If you personally do not have debt, you may know many others who do, and by helping them through this process, you help all of us to live in a better society.

Step 1. Create a Debt Elimination Box

List all your consumer debt. Like your Financial Baseline items, this should be done electronically so you can keep track easily. This list should include all of your credit cards, charge accounts, any high-interest loans that are not against an asset, and other outstanding credit or liabilities. The list should include (1) the name of the creditor, (2) the amount you owe, (3) minimum monthly payments, and (4) the interest rate.

NAME	AMOUNT	MINIMUM PAYMENT	INTEREST RATE	FACTORING #

On our Web site, www.liveoutloud.com, we have a debt calculator that allows you to insert these numbers and easily create these calculations.

Step 2. The Factoring Number

To fill in the last column, the factoring number, the following simple calculation is necessary. Take the number in column 2, which is the amount of the debt, and divide that number by the number in column 3, which is the minimum monthly payment required. For example, if you owe $7,000 on your credit card and the minimum monthly payment is $200, your factoring number would be 35. Fill in the factoring number for each item on your consumer debt list.

Step 3. Priority Payoff Box

On a new list, take the debt with the lowest factoring number and put it at the top. This debt is the first priority payoff. Continue to list the debt in order of the factoring number, with the debt with the lowest factoring number appearing in first place, the debt with the second lowest factoring number in second place, all the way down to the debt with the highest factoring number listed at the bottom.

ORDER OF PAYOFF	NAME OF DEBT	FACTORING #	MINIMUM PAYMENT
1.			
2.			
3.			
4.			
5.			
6.			

TOTAL DEBT PAYMENT: $_____

Step 4. The Jump-Start Allocation

In addition to the minimum payments required, you are going to take $200 from your current spending and allocate this to your debt elimination plan. This amount, about $7 a day, will greatly accelerate your debt elimination plan. Don't scream. This is going to be easier than you think. And once you put together your detailed Financial Baseline you will have a clear understanding of where your money comes from and where your money goes. Finding that $200 will not be difficult, and your cashflow from new assets may create the extra money. In my experience, when you list every single expenditure in your Financial Baseline, you will find a cut that doesn't even come close to forcing you to scrimp or sacrifice.

On the Financial Baseline of one of my clients, I discovered $600 a month spent on sushi. After several attempts to defend this expenditure, she finally, reluctantly, painstakingly, made a decision to spend just $400 a month on sushi. My guess is that when you honestly dig up your expenditures, you'll discover a few sushi-like items that you could, perhaps, not do away with altogether but cut down on a bit. For those of you still smoking, you can kill two birds with one stone: take care of your health and your wealth by cutting out cigarettes.

Step 5. Debt Payments

Take the debt listed in the first spot of the priority payoff box and apply the $200 jump-start allocation to the minimum payment listed with this debt. For example, if the minimum payment is $350, add the $200 for a new monthly payment of $550. While you continue to pay the normal monthly minimum payments on all the other debts, you will pay, in this example, $550 monthly on this specific debt until it is paid in full. When you're finished paying off the debt in the number one spot, you will take the amount you paid for those minimum monthly payments, plus the jump-start allocation, in our example $550, and add this amount, $550, to the minimum payment on the debt in the second slot. As you can see, the payments build and build as you drop on down the list of debts and your capacity to pay off your debt accelerates incrementally. Though you will be uncomfortable with this process at first, when you witness the speed at which you make progress, debt elimination will become as addictive as accumulating the debt once was.

In this plan, it is vital that you commit to making the minimum payments, and also to adding the jump-start allocation. That number, the jump-start allocation, must be specific and consistent. Additionally, you must have in your mindset that as you pay off one debt, the minimum payments stay in this debt payment pool and contribute to the next debt's payments. That is the only way this will work. And it works wonderfully well. You will be amazed at the speed with which you cross off each debt payment. And by the time you get to the one at the bottom, the one with the highest factoring number, which in reality represents the months it should take to pay it based on the original monthly payment, you'll see that you'll pay that debt off much faster than the factoring number indicated.

Making these commitments is tough to do on your own. I strongly recommend that you share your priority payoff box with members of your team. At times, you'll be tempted to use your credit cards or assume some additional debt. If your close friends and advisors have been given permission to check in with you about your debt, they will facilitate your process with a system of checks and balances against your old impulses.

Other Factors

As you make your way through the debt elimination process, you might also find ways to shrink some of the debt. One way would be to study the personal and business Financial Baselines you'll establish. Debt is a necessary part of building a business, and in many cases, the interest is tax-deductible as an expense against your revenues. When you shift some of your personal debt into your business Financial Baseline, you may discover that debt is in fact an expense against your revenue. If that's the case, that means your cash flow will increase. By reacquainting yourself with your tax structure, you may take a first step to shrinking your debt by increasing the cash you can use to pay off that debt. Additionally, you might consider talking to creditors and negotiating for lower interest payments. Most creditors are open to communication and will work with you to restructure your debt in a positive, progressive manner.

Back to Chuck's Wealth Plan

"By ignoring my debt, I actually made it bigger," Chuck said. "And now that my wealth is going up and my debt is going down, I'm feeling in control of my financial situation, and I'm realizing just how much anxiety ignoring all that debt was giving me."

And once you start to manage and aggressively diminish your debt, you will find that you too will take a lot of stress out of your life. Instead of constantly worrying about the money, the debt, and the credit cards, you will be freed up to think about other important things, like the acceleration of a successful Wealth Cycle Process.

"I'm in control of my debt, instead of it being in control of me," Chuck said. "And now that I'm in the driver's seat, Loral, I'm never going to give up that seat."

With each $3,000 monthly payment that Chuck made to pay off his debt, he made a contribution to his Wealth Account. He was also able to set up a holding account, or a corporate Wealth Account, in his business's S corp and in the LLC. He put $1,500 into each of these and $1,000 into his personal Wealth Account, for a total of $4,000 a month.

As the Cash Machine generated more income, and the Wealth Account began to grow, and Chuck was able to retain more of his earnings because of his entities and forecasting, he was able to start considering his *Assets* building block. Given that Chuck had no real assets to reallocate, we would use the money he was generating from his Cash Machine to create assets. After his tutoring company was up and running for a few months, Chuck had enough in his Wealth Accounts to buy one small cash flow–producing property in the Midwest. It was then his objective to purchase one house, every other month, for a total of six houses over the next 12 months.

ONE-YEAR FREEDOM DAY GOALS
- *$50,000 of invested assets*
- *$1,000/month cash flow*
- *Debt plan in place and actively managed*
- *Business directive to create Cash Machine*

REVENUE	**ASSETS**
CASH MACHINE	**FROM WEALTH ACCOUNT:**
TUTORING BUSINESS: *$10,000/month*	• *$6,000 for one bread-and-butter cash flow house*
PASSIVE INCOME: *$200/month*	• *$200/month CF*

FINANCIAL BASELINE

PRETAX INCOME: *$3,333/month*	**ASSETS:** *$7,000*
EXPENDITURES: *$4,000/month*	**LIABILITIES:** *$50,000*

SKILL SET: *Teaching, organization, enthusiasm, leadership, communication*

- *$5,000 teacher's pension*
- *$2,000 in cash*
- *$30,000 in consumer debt*
- *$20,000 in student loans*

Through his action, Chuck changed his Conditioning and came to realize that no matter how much money he made, and debt he had, he could still invest and build wealth. He also learned that he had a much greater capacity to make money than he thought possible. Chuck's approach to his Cash Machine was inspiring, even to him, and his success gave him the confidence to grow the business even bigger and really accelerate his Wealth Cycle.

Chuck had surrounded himself with others in debt, as well as those who made little money. He traded up to find a millionaire mentor who helped him collect the right professionals to support his wealth-building process, and fully committed to the Teamwork and Leadership needed to be successful. Only 30 and unsure that his chosen profession was going to satisfy him in the long run, Chuck had put himself in a good position to make the choices toward a more fulfilling life.

Removing the Greatest Barrier to Wealth

Building wealth from a position of great debt takes courage, discipline, and positive energy. I realize this is a difficult scenario from which to create wealth, but I also know that getting out of debt and building wealth is very doable. Chuck Wallace is just one of many clients with whom I've worked who had a lot of debt, no assets, and limited income. But by focusing on the Cash Machine and retaining those new earnings through entities, Chuck, and many clients like him, become more conscious of spending and more focused in their determination to put dollars into the Wealth Account and manage their lifestyle. In time, this leads to the capacity to eliminate debt, build assets, and enjoy a lifetime of your money making money for you.

Seven Wealth Cycles

"The way you put the building blocks of the Wealth Cycle together almost seems like a game," the television producer said. After the Leonard family's case study I had walked her through the six case studies you just read.

"It's very much like a strategic game," I said. "Anyone can take these 12 building blocks and figure out their route to wealth. It's not that hard. They just need to figure out how to do the right thing at the right time."

"I think I'm Rick Noonan," she said. "I'm just sitting on a big house in Winnetka, Illinois, and I have a lot of stock options in the network I work for."

"That could be," I said.

"And my sister is definitely Kerry Kingsley," she said. "I've got to talk to her about her companies. You've never seen anyone with more businesses and less money than her. I certainly know the Joneses; they live all around my neighborhood and my best friend is Chuck Wallace for sure. . . ."

Through the case studies I've shared with you so far, you've seen how the six middle steps of the building blocks are used in a variety of sequences, depending on each person's requirements and objectives.

Forecasting	Entities
Assets	Cash Machine
Wealth Account	Debt Management

At this point, you may be able to identify with one of the scenarios I presented:

1. The Leonard family, threatened by a job loss

   Gap Analysis → Financial Baseline → Freedom Day

   Assets → Cash Machine → Entities → Forecasting → Debt Management → Wealth Account

   Teamwork + Conditioning + Leadership

2. Rick Noonan with his badly invested assets

   Gap Analysis → Financial Baseline → Freedom Day

   Assets → Entities → Forecasting → Wealth Account → Cash Machine → Debt Management

   Teamwork + Conditioning + Leadership

3. Patricia Beasley, straddler, business as a hobby

   Gap Analysis → Financial Baseline → Freedom Day

   Cash Machine → Entities → Forecasting → Wealth Account → Assets → Debt Management

   Leadership + Conditioning + Teamwork

4. Kerry Kingsley, business owner, not enough income

   Gap Analysis → Financial Baseline → Freedom Day

   Entities → Forecasting → Cash Machine → Wealth Account → Assets → Debt Management

   Leadership + Conditioning + Teamwork

5. Jim Quinlin, victim of taxable money

Gap Analysis → Financial Baseline → Freedom Day

Forecasting → Cash Machine → Debt Management
→ Wealth Account → Assets → Entities

Conditioning + Teamwork + Leadership

6. Jean and John Jones, big leased lifestyle

Gap Analysis → Financial Baseline → Freedom Day

Entities → Forecasting → Assets → Wealth Account
→ Cash Machine → Debt Management

Leadership + Conditioning + Teamwork

7. Chuck Wallace, big debt

Gap Analysis → Financial Baseline → Freedom Day

Cash Machine → Entities → Forecasting →
Debt Management → Wealth Account → Assets

Conditioning + Teamwork + Leadership

As I mentioned before, each of the middle building blocks in the Wealth Cycle Process has an intention and purpose, yet each can be utilized and emphasized in a variety of ways, depending on the scenario. But all wealth plans in the Wealth Cycle Process, regardless of the individual wealth builder, begin with the first three blocks—

Gap Analysis, Financial Baseline, and Freedom Day—and are dependent on the last three blocks—Leadership, Teamwork, and Conditioning.

Now it's time to discuss exactly what that financial Gap Analysis is made of so that you can get down to business and begin to create your own wealth plan.

Getting to
the bottom to
get to the top . . .

10

YOUR FINANCIAL BASELINE
Walk the Beans

I f you don't know what it means to "walk the beans," you're lucky. That was one of the many chores my four siblings and I had to do during the long summer days on our parents' Nebraska farm. That meant that you had to walk the rows of beans and pluck the weeds from between and around each and every stalk. That, I tell you, was a tedious chore.

But, it did keep the beans growing, which kept clothes on our backs and food on the table. So maybe it's from walking the beans that I find it satisfying to get my hands back in the roots once in a while. Even if the work is as tedious as walking the beans, as long as that digging leads to growth, it's okay.

With any luck, that little parable will get you inspired to dig through your files and begin your Financial Baseline. As you saw in each of the case studies, the Financial Baseline is a summary of your current financial situation. As with the Leonards, Rick Noonan,

Patricia Beasley, and the others, you may find that what surfaces is not appealing. It doesn't matter. I say, "So what? Now what?" It's time to move ahead. The point of the Financial Baseline is to know where you are so that you can get to where you're going.

Those who've followed this proprietary process say that this step is probably the toughest step in the plan. It's not mind-bending, but it can be a bit wearisome. Believe me, it is well worth the effort, because (1) it's a one-time exercise, and once the system is maintained, the heavy-lifting aspect will not be repeated, and (2) once done, the walk out of the desert to the water is a great deal easier.

You might even consider making this activity more of a group event by finding like-minded friends and scheduling a day to do this exercise together. This is a good way to begin creating your Team-Made Millionaire community. But whether you do it alone or as a group event, don't delay. Get into this exercise immediately. The sooner you do it, the sooner it's done, and you will soar to a whole new level of action.

Clarifying your Financial Baseline is unique to our approach. Few programs are willing to ask you to do this step because they fear you will lose interest and quit altogether. But I know their fear is unfounded because every single person in our Team-Made Millionaire community has accomplished this task and when you do it, you too will surge forward and begin to change your current situation and step toward wealth.

There are two parts to determining your Financial Baseline. The first is the Financial Filing Cabinet; the second is the Real Financial Statements.

The Financial Filing Cabinet

We all have financial papers, such as bank statements, credit card statements, and personal receipts. But many of us have these lying about in shoeboxes or stacked in an envelope or stuffed into a drawer . . . if we're lucky.

Believe it or not, cleaning up this mess will begin to change your life. It is essential and, if you gloss over it on your way to the big fun stuff, you will find that your new paint will peel fast. Roll up your sleeves; clarity is waiting.

A note about commingling personal and business finances: You shall commingle no more. It's time to move up to the Big Table—to be a grown-up and run your business as a business and your personal life as your personal life. As we set up entities for each of your businesses, the line between your worlds will be drawn even more clearly. If you have a business, or a household with two income-producing adults, proceed through these steps separately for each one. It's time to un-commingle.

Step 1: Dig out your papers and disengage emotionally. The key here is to remind yourself that these pieces of paper represent your past. Sorting through them is a step into your future.

Step 2: Organize your Financial Filing Cabinet by spreading out your papers and sorting them into the following categories: bank statements; credit card statements; receipts and cash expenses; all of your personal and professional overhead expenses, including utilities: gas, electric, water, phone, both landline and cell, Internet services, etc.; insurance policies for home, life, car, etc.; wills; retirement planning documents; college and education funds; investment portfolios; real estate documents; and other papers regarding the money that comes in and out of your life.

Step 3: Create a filing system to track your monthly revenue, including income and expenditures. This means setting up individual files for each item:

Bank statements

Active income wages and
 salaries

Stocks and bonds

Real estate holdings

Entities, trusts, and estates

Credit card statements

Receipts/cash expenses

Power and water bills

Phone bills (land and cell)

Internet services

Insurance policies

Wills

Retirement planning

Education funds

Other

Set up files for all of these items and remember to keep separate files for personal income and expenses and business revenue and expenditures. Even if you don't have any entities now, you will as the process continues. It is a good idea to make copies of your important documents—for example, wills, trusts, deeds, and stock certificates. File the copies and store the original documents in a safe deposit box.

Step 4: Good record keeping is an essential part of sound financial management. Make the following list of all of your important documents and account numbers and their locations.

	DOCUMENT	ACCT NO. OR NAME	LOCATION
GENERAL			
BIRTH CERTIFICATES			
MARRIAGE CERTIFICATES			
SOCIAL SECURITY CARD			
DIVORCE DECREE			
PASSPORT			
POWERS OF ATTORNEY			
FINANCIAL			
HEALTH			

LIVING WILL			
WILL			
TRUST AGREEMENTS			
INSURANCE POLICIES			
LIFE			
HEALTH			
DISABILITY			
HOMEOWNER'S/RENTER'S			
AUTO			
EMPLOYEE BENEFIT DATA			
GROUP INSURANCE			
PENSION PLAN			
SAVINGS/PROFIT SHARING			
BANKING RECORDS			
CHECKING			
SAVINGS			
BANK BOOKS			
CHECKING STATEMENTS			
CERTIFICATES			
SAFE DEPOSIT BOX KEY			
INVESTMENT RECORDS			
FINANCIAL STATEMENTS			
STOCK CERTIFICATES			
BOND CERTIFICATES			
INCOME TAX RECORDS			
CURRENT YEAR BACKUP			
PAST YEARS' FILES			
HOUSING RECORDS			
IMPROVEMENTS			
PROPERTY TAX PAYMENTS			
MORTGAGE PAYMENTS			
APPLIANCE WARRANTIES			
CREDIT CARD STATEMENTS			

These lists, one for each person and business, should be copied and given to your spouse, trusted friend, family member, attorney, or accountant. It is also essential to get your finances on the computer. There are plenty of good software programs that will track your revenues and expenditures as they come and go.

Your *REAL* Financial Statements

Given that I believe anyone who wants to build wealth should structure the financial aspects of their life in the same way that businesses structure their organizations, it should be no surprise to you that I think individuals should have their own financial statements.

The profit and loss statement provides a snapshot of income and expenses—and profitability. The balance sheet is a document that is split right down the middle; it shows the assets (what is owned) on the left, and the liabilities and equity (who owns it) on the right. The total of assets and the total of liabilities plus equity are always the same number; that is, they balance.

Revenue	Expenditures
Assets	Liabilities

As you can see, it is from these four interdependent blocks that we derive the information for the Financial Baseline of the Gap Analysis.

1. **Revenue.** The total amount of active and passive income you are taking in. This is bigger than your income, since it includes all cash from all your activities, before costs and expenditures, taxes,

interest, or any depreciation or amortization. Revenue is not the same as income: *revenue* means all the money that comes in; *income* means all the money that is left after the costs of making it are deducted.

2. **Expenditures.** This is all the money that is going out—the money that must be spent to maintain your life or your business. We are talking about real cash, hard dollars, flowing out. Not to be confused with *expenses*, which is an accounting term that includes things like depreciation, that is, accounting deductions where real cash is not going out.

3. **Assets.** Everything you own.

4. **Liabilities.** Everything you owe.

Create Financial Statements for your personal life and for each one of your businesses. If yours is a two-family income, list each person's income and expenses separately within that one revenue and expenditures block, because you may be affected by or liable for the other person's finances.

If you don't already have one, open a bank account for your business. You'll need to make sure your business is properly organized according to your state's requirements. Your bank will tell you exactly what you need to do this, and a quick search on the Internet will help you find the right forms. If this feels too complicated, then hold off for now, until you get some help from an accountant, mentor, or coach to create your entities. But do keep separate Financial Statements for each business now.

The Profit and Loss Statement

These top two boxes are where you fill in the answers to Questions 1 and 2 of the Gap Analysis: "What is your monthly income?" and "What are your monthly expenditures?"

You should list your incoming cash—your revenue—in the revenue box on the left side, and your outgoing cash— your expenditures—in the expenditure box on the right side.

- Include *all* your income, both active and passive, and *all* your expenditures, including the latest accessory you bought or the sandwich you get every day from the deli.
- Be detailed. If in doubt, do not leave it out.
- If your revenue or income fluctuates, use a 90-day average. If it varies wildly, use a 6-month average.
- Include taxes, and the work to get them done, in the expenditure column.

If you're having trouble separating your business and personal statements, consider that the following might be business expenditures:

- office or home office deduction
- utilities, phone, and automobile deductions
- entertainment
- meals
- insurance payments
- office supplies
- computer equipment
- education
- accounting, bookkeeping, and legal fees
- gifts
- staff
- travel
- gas
- salaries, including those of family members who work in the business

Once you've listed all your revenue and all your expenditures, do the math and calculate the positive or negative cash amount.

The Balance Sheet

The two bottom squares are where you answer Questions 3 and 4 of the Gap Analysis: "What assets do you have?" and "What are your liabilities?" This will reveal two things: your net worth and your financial habits and tendencies. Again, we're going to separate any business financials from personal ones, so make sure you are entering the proper assets and liabilities for this particular Financial Statement.

List your assets (the things you own and the things that have value to you) on the left in the box marked Assets. List each of your liabilities (money owed to banks, credit card companies, individuals, etc.) separately on the right in the box marked Liabilities. A traditional balance sheet would include equity—the amount that you own outright—but we're going to calculate this as your net worth, when you subtract the liabilities from the assets. For some of you, the net worth may be zero or a negative number, but once you're in the Wealth Cycle Process that will change.

After you've filled in these four boxes, you need to go to Question 5 of the Gap Analysis and ask yourself, "What else?" Make sure there are no orphan IRAs or small loans from Uncle Joe that you need to include.

Now that you've answered Questions 1 to 5 of the Gap Analysis and filled in the Financial Baseline with the numbers from your REAL Financial Statements, you might have an idea of how your building blocks need to be sequenced. For example, if your Financial Baseline reveals that you don't make and retain enough income, you have to begin your building blocks with Cash Machine, then Entities, followed by Forecasting, Wealth Account, Assets, and

Debt Management. If your Financial Baseline reveals overwhelming debt, then you need to consider a sequence that starts with the Wealth Account, followed by Debt Management, Cash Machine, Entities, Forecasting, and then Assets. If you noticed you have a lot of income but little cash on hand and many underperforming assets, you need to start with the Assets building block, followed by the Cash Machine, Entities, Forecasting, Wealth Account, and Debt Management.

The Financial Baseline assessment is critical. It can also be somewhat intense and emotional. But once it's completed, it is a lot easier to maintain, either by yourself or with the help of a bookkeeper, and you are well on your way to generating your wealth.

What do you want?

11

FINANCIAL FREEDOM DAY
See the Money

Question 6 of the Gap Analysis asks, "What do you want?"
The first step on this road to making you a millionaire is to create and clarify your vision. Before you start, you might want to ask yourself why you are doing this. A vision is big. It's bigger than a goal, and it's bigger than an objective. For example, an objective is to get out of debt. A goal might be to buy the new car or pay for the kids to go to college. But a vision is the greater umbrella under which all these goals and objectives come together, through specific strategies that support the vision and tactics that support those strategies. Understanding what a vision means, and really wanting that vision, is important. If you're just out to buy a new boat, then this book is too big for you and I may have you go in a direction that, ultimately, you don't want to go. It's your job to consider where it is you want to go.

I'll help you see your vision by sharing with you my vision for you in reading this book.

The Vision: Financial freedom. The capacity to have your assets generate enough cash flow to maintain a superior standard of living that supports the optimal life you want to live forever.

The Strategy: I will help you create assets and generate wealth, incrementally and in some cases exponentially. The wealth will come to legal entities from multiple revenue streams generated by your assets.

The Tactics: By using the right sequence of building blocks, you will take a systematic, practical, and tactical approach to create and continuously increase your wealth. If you have any questions on your sequence or your approach, please feel free to call my Strategists at any time. As I've mentioned, wealth building is a team sport, and I want my team to get bigger and bigger.

I agree with the philosophers who say the journey is its own reward, because I know that once you're fully into this one, it will become a lifelong compulsion and desire. But I also believe that the journey will be most rewarding if there is a specific point to which your compass is set. It is your responsibility to clarify your vision. It will help you better embrace the time and effort you are going to put into this commitment.

In order to keep you motivated, the vision needs three key components. It must be exciting enough to fuel your energies, reasonable enough to be doable, and it must never compromise your values. It's a balancing act between your ultimate wish list, perhaps even the dream you put aside when you were a child, and your life as it is, and has to be, at the moment.

When you create your vision, you have to exercise No-Limit Thinking. You have to imagine what your life would look like if it were impossible to fail. With this type of thinking, your vision will expand. We all have the capacity to be financially free. It's our responsibility to choose that course, to claim the power and get what we deserve: Financial Freedom Day.

Financial Freedom Day

This is why your vision is so important. People who lack a clear vision are like ships without rudders: they sail aimlessly and without a final destination. They may head toward opportunities that appear on the horizon, but then veer off course, unable to reach them.

Given that your vision is a concept or an idea, we need to quantify that vision with a measurable goal in order to best map out a strategic plan to get you there. As you saw in each of the case studies, in order to declare your Financial Freedom Day you need to decide

1. How much cash flow you need to receive each month
2. What you want your net worth to be
3. The specific day, month, and year you want this to occur

In order to answer these questions, we need to set financial goals. I know very well that if you start writing down numbers, they can get a bit discouraging. It's one thing to say that you'd like to have a net worth of $3 million and cash flow of $30,000 a month by the time you're 50 years old. But it's another to make those commitments and then look at where you are now. That gap can scare you away and make you abandon any vision, no matter how compelling. It is vital that at this point you see these numbers as reference points and measurements, and every hurdle as an opportunity to learn a new lesson and make a better choice.

It would be similar to the decision to walk from San Francisco to Washington, D.C. That's an exciting and doable objective. But even if you can manage 20 miles a day, it will still take half a year. The number of reference points you have to pass—each city and state along the way—and the hurdles you must overcome—bad weather, sore feet—may all seem daunting, but if you keep walking, you know you'll make it, because you've got your vision set for the nation's capital and the course is defined.

The first step is to list your general financial goals. These may include such ideas as starting your own business, living a life of luxury, creating a charity, or sending all your kids to college and graduate school. These are broad objectives that need to be sketched in greater detail. The second step is to think about exactly how much money you need in order to have that goal be reasonable.

First, list your broad objectives: for example, to have a net worth of over $10 million, annual cash flow of $2 million, and a home in San Francisco and Paris; to start a children's summer camp; and to make charitable contributions of, at least, $500,000 annually.

Next, evaluate and prioritize each of the goals in the broad objective. In doing so, you should take into account (1) its level of importance, (2) the time frame in which you want to accomplish each goal, and (3) the amount of money you think you'd need to accomplish that goal. When you create your Financial Baseline, you will see how much money you will need to get to each goal, based on your current financial situation.

The third step is to forecast how much you must invest each month to reach your financial goal. This number has nothing to do with taking care of debt and other obligations—not yet. We are working on your vision, where you want to go, and the specific actions to make this work will follow.

Let's say, for example, one of your goals is to put a child through college, fully covering tuition and books, as well as a monthly stipend for rent, clothing, food, a car, auto insurance, and some entertainment. Before we can determine how much you need to invest monthly to reach your goal, several variables must be filled in. These variables are time, total cost, rates of return, and the mathematical multiplier. (For this goal, college tuition and expenses, the variables can vary wildly. In the example, below, I'm using numbers that are realistic, but not necessarily based on any specific situation, college, or investment vehicle.)

Time: The time it will take to reach the goal: for example, 15 years

Total cost: Estimated cost of the goal: for example, $150,000

Rate of return: The monthly interest you can earn on investing cash now: for example, 6 percent

Mathematical multiplier: The number you multiply with your total cost

To find out how much you need to invest each month, you multiply the total cost of your goal by the mathematical multiplier (noted below). If you have the other two variables—total number of years to reach your goal and the rate of return (in this example, 15 years and 6 percent), you can quickly get the mathematical multiplier from any bank, financial Web site, or financial software program such as Quicken and Excel.

The mathematical multiplier for 15 years at 6 percent is 0.0034. The equation looks like this:

$$\$150,000 \times 0.0034 = \$510 \text{ per month}$$

You can use the mathematical worksheet on our Web site, www.liveoutloud.com, to find the multiplier for each of your goals, inputting the number of years and the amount of interest you're going to use. The chart will help you work these out.

STATE BROAD OBJECTIVE

PRIORITIZE EACH GOAL

1.

2.

3.

CALCULATE GOAL INVESTMENT PLAN

1. GOAL NO. 1

TIME REQUIRED TO REACH GOAL:

TOTAL COST TO REACH GOAL:

RATE OF RETURN:

MONTHLY INVESTMENT REQUIRED.

2. GOAL NO. 2

TIME REQUIRED TO REACH GOAL:

TOTAL COST TO REACH GOAL:

RATE OF RETURN:

MONTHLY INVESTMENT REQUIRED.

3. GOAL NO. 3

TIME REQUIRED TO REACH GOAL:

TOTAL COST TO REACH GOAL:

RATE OF RETURN:

MONTHLY INVESTMENT REQUIRED.

At this point, you have your financial goals, the priority of those goals, and how much cash it would take each month to make those goals come true. Let me assure you that there is every reason to believe you can do this. We're just going to do it—then you'll believe it.

With your Financial Baseline clarified, and your Freedom Day defined, you should answer Question 7: "What skills do you use to make money?" Add this to your Financial Baseline under Skill Set, as we did in the case studies. Now you're ready to lead your wealth.

The CEO of your life . . .

12

TEAMWORK AND LEADERSHIP
Team-Made Millionaires

As you saw in each case study, the three building blocks of Team-work, Leadership, and Conditioning support and drive the Wealth Cycle Process. It's important for you to reflect on each of these as you begin to consider your wealth plan.

There is no such thing as a self-made millionaire. It's just impossible to do without a peer-to-peer team of mentors, financiers, field partners, and colleagues. Team-Made Millionaires work for and with each other to generate wealth.

While working on the team, you should always be aware of what position you are playing and when. In your personal wealth-building efforts, you must never, ever give anyone else permission to lead you, abdicate your leadership role, or release responsibility or accountability on any decision. You are the leader of your own wealth. And as long as you remain aware of the fact that the final responsibilities and accountabilities are yours, you can listen to others' advice and take their suggestions. This includes mentors and coaches who might ask you to take on the discomfort of change that is necessary for your growth. If you assume responsibility and you have chosen coaches whom you feel you can trust absolutely, then you can allow yourself to surrender to their suggestions, take the actions they prescribe, get uncomfortable, and grow. The best leaders are great followers because they know where they are going and they trust themselves enough to find good leaders to help get them there.

In our Team-Made Millionaire community, one in which we hope you'll be a part, you might hear us ask one another who wants to play. We use the word *play* because making money is fun. We all take wealth building very seriously, but many people on my team have enough to live on for years to come, and our children are well taken care of. Investing is an exciting and fun world in which to play, and none of us are ever going to stop looking for the bigger, better game. Ask any investment banker, portfolio manager, or trader what a good day is and he or she will tell you the ins and outs and excitement of a deal. Believe me, it's the fun and excitement, even more than the money, that keeps my wealth team completely engaged.

If it weren't a satisfying game, my team wouldn't still be helping me and I wouldn't still be helping them. Just as I've captured others with my vision, they've captured me with theirs. In my wealth-building community, it's about all of us, together.

It's imperative that you assemble a great team of great people whom you can lead to your success. The reality is, in today's complex, fast-paced world, few people have the time or talent to do everything expertly themselves, even if they want to. You may be the most far-seeing visionary, brilliant deal maker, toughest negotiator, and finest closer, but you may not be an inspired tax wizard, legal genius, or office manager.

Finding a Mentor

Getting a mentor is a vital first step to building your wealth. If you're floundering about in frustration or operating in a community that offers less support than it does hindrance, you want to pursue a mentor soon.

Finding a mentor can be easy for some and harder for others. If you are one of the lucky few who have the person you admire most presiding in the house next door, go knock on that door. But if, as is more likely, your community or immediate neighborhood is bereft of those in the bigger, better world to which you aspire, you need to reach out a little further. Team-Made Millionaires are made through networking and contacts and creating a community of mentors, leaders, and fellow visionaries. Here are some things to keep in mind and ways to find a mentor.

Communicate Your Ambition

You'll discover that just by talking and sharing your vision with others, you will start to generate forward motion. Of the many people you talk to about your vision, or just your desire to have a bigger and better vision, if one of them can advise you on that vision or can connect you to someone who can, that's a big step into a better and bigger network.

Cull All Your Resources

Think hard. Consider people who share a connection with you through your hometown, your school, or a friend of a friend. Pick up the phone and give the person a call. The worst case, he or she will be flattered and say no.

Stretch with Specific Intention

Your Uncle Joe may be the smartest, nicest guy in the world, but if he doesn't have at least a million dollars, then he's not your mentor for wealth building. Remember, this team is to build your wealth; that is its specific intention and goal. And because kindness and wealth are not mutually exclusive virtues, we suggest you find someone who has both. It doesn't behoove you, or your conscience, to make good money with bad company.

The Most Special Can Be the Most Subtle

Most wealth in this country is inconspicuous. Do your research. The man down the street driving the nice car and living in the mansion could easily have greater debt and a lower net worth than the stealthy and wealthy plumber who drives a beat-up truck but seems to work only when he doesn't feel like fishing.

Be Persuasive and Persistent, but Not Pesky

Once you find your way in through the myriad of inevitable guard dogs, you need to take action that will show the mentor you will do what it takes to be coached by him or her. I've had many mentors in many industries throughout my life and my approach to getting to them has always been somewhat similar.

In an example that preceded my current goal in my larger vision, I called a nationally renowned wealth-building speaker and told him I wanted to work with him. After finally getting him on the phone in person, he told me to send him a letter of intent. Though others may have waited for the letter to arrive and for him to respond, I hung up the phone, wrote the letter, put it in the mail and called him an hour later. I told him I'd done that and asked what was next. He sighed and told me that if I were really interested I could get on a plane and go talk to him. I did, and ended up working with him for several years, helping him to build his business and his reputation, as well as my knowledge base and my list of what I did and did not want to do.

Most people talk, but few people act, and the best mentors can sense the difference between someone who is pushy and someone who is committed. If you have a vision, you have to show up for that vision, and that means getting committed to getting a mentor.

Do Not Accept a Scripted Mentor

There are several financial infomercials currently running that will suggest you call one of their "standing by" coaches, ready to help you move forward. I know, from experience, that these coaches sit in one telephone center where they read scripts and recite answers to frequently asked questions. This is absolutely not acceptable. You need a coach who will speak specifically to you, tailoring the advice to your particular needs, wants, and situation.

The mentor can be the first member of your team, but like all the personnel you gather, there will most likely be a constant influx and outflow of players.

Gathering the Team

That's definitely been the case with me as my life and decisions change in advance of my bigger vision. Building a great team takes some experience, which includes making some mistakes. Since you need to build the team before you have much experience you should prepare yourself for some conflicts. With the help of your mentor or mentors, you should be able to find the right people. For example, given that your mentor should be at least a millionaire, he or she should have a good accountant who can either help you or recommend someone good in the field.

My team is made up of both Strategic Partners and an in-house management group, circling the hub of my ultimate vision. And as the vision grows and changes, my team spreads out in both concentric and interlinking circles, like the Big Tables in our Team-Made Millionaire community, creating not just one but several great teams working within this larger community of people who are eager to live out loud and build their wealth.

Design Your Business Divorce While You're Still in Love

Because life has a tendency to be unpredictable, both plans and people have a tendency to change. That's why I always suggest that in any business relationship you design your divorce while you're still in love. For those of you with relationship experience, this pretty much speaks for itself. We've all been through painful break-ups, both personal and professional, and we all know these are not times when people are at their most rational.

A few years ago, a woman I was working with on a business venture died unexpectedly. She'd left her piece of our pie to her young boyfriend, who didn't play well with others but had no desire to let go of his shares. He inherited the business and we inherited him—and the entire team of first-rate Strategic Partners suffered for this one rotten apple. Eventually, we finally agreed to our only viable exit, and that was to reluctantly sell the business. Subsequent to that experience I have never gone into another business relationship without a right to purchase the participation of a shareholder upon death or divorce.

Players to Be Named

A good team should have the following players:

1. Mentors who act as active coaches
2. Like-minded, supportive wealth builders and visionaries
3. Top-rate industry- or task-specific legal counsel
4. Accountants
5. Leading-edge, nontraditional financial experts, such as an IRA expert

Optimally, a good team should also have

1. A business broker who can scout out private placement, leveraged buyout, and franchise and licensing opportunities
2. Various real estate players, including commercial and residential brokers, project scouts and managers, contractors, builders, and developers
3. Others who know investment opportunities

If you own and run a business, your team will possibly need professionals in

1. Marketing
2. Publicity
3. Finance
4. Operations
5. Channels/distribution

And, of course, every team needs utility players to function as in-house management. These should consist of

1. Administrators
2. Assistants
3. Bookkeepers
4. Graphic designers
5. Writers
6. Financial analysts
7. Office managers
8. Computer support personnel
9. Technical advisors
10. Sales reps
11. Marketing professionals

Finding the personal support crew to help you focus more time on your wealth, your health, and your family should begin as soon as possible. It is imperative that whatever team you assemble be a team that will buy into your vision and take action to meet that vision. The team has to act; it cannot just talk or stall in analysis paralysis. Or you'll be a whole lot wiser, but not a lot wealthier.

Getting the Bigger, Better Brain

The first step is to discover the players in the field. Figure out their names, their areas of expertise, and their special talent. Round up recommendations from people you respect about those with whom they've worked and then find a way to reach the latter. Approach the wealthiest, most successful, and well-connected people you know; ask them who they use and if they would be willing to make introductions for you.

As you start to attract the best and brightest to your team, it might be difficult to first create access and then afford them. But it will be well worth your time and your effort. I've found that the inexpensive and easily accessible professionals often prove to be far more expensive in the long run. Wealthy people and wealth-building professionals know that time is money, and they tend to cut right to the chase. They've already spent years learning the ropes and exactly where to go and have usually figured out the best routes. Frequently, they can do more with a single phone call than others can produce in months of diligent effort. Additionally, the top experts are usually close to the inner circle of motion and action. They know the latest industry buzz and developments, the top deal and the dealmakers, and what's currently being pursued and what's needed in that pursuit.

If you build a reputation for working only with the best, then only the best will want to work with you. Top people can put you into lucrative investments that you might never find on your own, and they can advise you on whom to avoid and when to pass on an opportunity, which can save you a lot of time, money, and frustration. Top talent will also connect you with other top talent and open up doors that otherwise might be closed. Experts know other experts, and have contacts who can raise the level of your game. They can move you up to the bigger and more profitable leagues where the players are in for higher stakes.

When you build a great team and work with the best, you can't help but improve your own proficiency, the speed and efficiency with which you fast-forward your growth, and the extent to which the work becomes more fulfilling and enjoyable. Working with the best will motivate you to reach new heights.

As you know, there's usually no need to reinvent the wheel. Whatever you hope to accomplish has most likely been done in one form or another. You should take the time to find a mentor who has done some variation of your vision rather than impede and slow your progress by trying to be clever and go it alone. Experience and know-how are invaluable, as are contacts and networks. Speed your growth by tapping into the growth of others and hitching on to the ride.

If you're not sure what your utility positions are, remember that as the team leader you are always leading your team to the vision, the strategies that support that vision, and then down into the tactics. These tactics become the job descriptions for your utility players.

Utility players are as crucial and indispensable to the team as the franchise players, whom I call my Strategic Partners, and, like the franchise players, the best are usually the best. These people provide the logistics and support services you need to make each goal, and ultimately your vision, happen. If you are currently handling all the logistics in your life and your business, you may be holding yourself back.

In wealth building there is no special prize for martyrs or people who believe they can do it all. Though you or others may see you as Superman or Wonder Woman, and though you really might have many of their super and wonderful powers, you also live in the real world, where there are only 168 hours in the week.

Think about all the great ways you could be making money if you did not spend time doing work that others could do for you. Just as you took the time to look at where you're spending your money every month, it is important that you take a look at where you are spending your time. You may discover that there are many tasks that literally rob you of hours you could better spend on your wealth-building efforts.

The best of the best, both the utility and franchise players, will join your team if they feel it's going to be successful. Many people want to be a part of something great, and if you are leading toward greatness, many people will want to go with you.

Assuring Accountability

In working with a team, you need to create accountability through action. Progress is made faster when everyone is on the same page and knows what is expected. Your wealth team will be more efficient if the measurable results of any action are clear. It's essential to set up tracking for any project or task you request from a wealth team member. Remember, the more efficient you are, the better use you'll make of everyone's time—which will save you money.
Here's a formula I've found that works. List:

1. The task to be completed
2. The time or date it will be completed
3. The people who will complete it
4. The person who will enforce the accountability for its completion

The last step is not to be skipped. To support your goals, and keep your team focused and on track, you need to establish accountability partners. These partners will lend their support to assure that the mission is accomplished as planned and scheduled. It's a bit like a professional nag, only you take it better when they say, "I know you are committed to finish project A, and the deadline is quickly approaching." The accountability partner should then ask you to share, step-by-step, the tasks you still need to complete, help you, if necessary, renegotiate with your team to get the work done, and support and help you in any additional ways.

Accountability partners support; they do not blame. There should be no fall guys. In accountability partnerships, the questioner's main goal is to prompt and support the partner's intention. It's a type of internal review that keeps team members focused and on track. When team players take an active interest in outcomes, it gives the people doing the heavy lifting a support system.

As you move forward, you're also going to need a lifeline for your psychology. Make sure someone you trust and respect is on the other end of that phone.

A Good Leader and Team Player

A leader leads through inspiration. People like to work with people going places and are starved for the energy and excitement that business was always meant to have. As a good leader, you want to fill your team with other leaders. Again, this doesn't mean your team will have a dozen chefs and no choppers. It means that the team will be composed of strong characters who know how to play their position and play it well, to the benefit of the team and themselves.

You do not manage a wealth team, you lead it. Select franchise and utility players who are self-managers. If you have to micromanage you are defeating the purpose and wasting valuable time. All the players on your team should be excited by your vision and energized by your pursuit. And since you will provide them with fair participation in deals, or pay them well for their services, they will be eager to serve you in the best way possible.

Leadership breeds a cooperative, self-propelling team. If someone on your team seems overbearing or puts down your vision, do what I do: trade up. It's a waste of everyone's time to keep people on board who are not on board. It's not fair to you or the other members of the team. There are several qualities of leadership that I believe to be the thrust of a good wealth builder.

Intuition: Listening to the Room

Intuition is the one leadership quality we were all born with and which we somehow lost along the way. In order to be an effective wealth builder, you've got to bring your intuition back home. Most of the time, you know you're in the ballpark, you can feel it in your gut, but you don't have the courage to speak your convictions. When I want to respond to the general vibe in the room, the thing that I know will make or break a deal, I use the phrasing "I sense this." It allows me to speak to what I'm hearing in the room. Because, really, that's what intuition is—the highest form of listening.

There are three levels of listening. Most people live at level one. Leaders need to live at level three. Level one listeners listen to themselves, as well as the conditioning voices in their head and the mass of stimuli and impressions blasting at them daily. I think 80 percent of the planet lives here, in this loud, chaotic place, constantly reacting, busy, but unproductive. Level two listening is when you are captured contently in a conversation with others, engaged, involved, completely in the moment and connected. Level three listening is intuition. It's when you have your arms around the entire room, listening to everything that is going on everywhere. It's a calm listening that goes beyond words, where you actually use all the resources that surround you to anticipate what will happen. At level three listening, even in the speed of events, there is a steadiness where you have access to the message of what is really happening, you know what you know.

In these situations you'll see that good leaders, looking at numbers that work and operations that seem flawless, make the final decision based on their gut. This skill of using intuition comes from the subconscious, but it can be improved through awareness and experience.

Self-Management

Despite claims to the contrary, in getting things done, time management is not the issue. It's really a matter of activity and energy management, that is, highest, best use of time. As I've said, it's doing the right thing at the right time. This requires

Sequencing. Seeing the best next steps can be the most important quality of a good leader. Too many people get all muddled in the process and bogged down with the details, or they get deluded by the vision and walk about thinking big airy thoughts. A leader must have the ability to know what step to take when. But even leaders get lost in the muck at times, and that's why a great leader has great mentors and coaches who know when to say "Whoa, wait a moment, here you go." Circles are nice in geometry, but wealth builders look for straight lines.

Timelines. In order to reach your goals, you need nonnegotiable timelines. I usually work with 120-day goals, counting backward—which means tomorrow is day 119. Believe me, that gets you going.

Seeing real reward. The ability to see if each idea, or even each step, truly has, or will lead to, profit potential is crucial. Ideas flow easily, but doing the work to make them happen is a whole other thing. It's not worth the effort if there's no reward at the end, and a good leader should know if there is or is not potential for that reward.

Catalyzing. Leaders have to be so certain about their sequencing capacity that they can insert suggestions or do tasks that serve as a catalyst to get things done. Sometimes, leaders will notice that everyone is doing his or her part, and doing it right, but in the wrong order. That's when they need to catalyze and make sure that the process gets in the right order. Catalyzing also means creating enrollment in the vision, seeing how people fit, and aligning them so they feel significant in their role. Using language like "working with me" rather than "working for me," as well as letting people play the position they request, usually helps to create enrollment.

Compartmentalization. Many of us have a tendency to bleed the consequences of one situation into another. You know what I'm talking about. It's 9 a.m., you have a meeting, the people you meet excite you about an idea or they anger you, you walk out of that situation, and into an 11 a.m. meeting, and that exciting news or conflict from the first situation follows you right into that next situation. And either you spend the first 15 minutes distracted about it or you share it with the new people you're with, but either way, the events of the 9 a.m. compartment have stolen minutes from the 11 a.m. compartment.

When you're in activation mode for wealth building, you need to be efficient and productive. You need to employ your self-management muscles and park the right issues in the right spots. Whatever it takes to do this, taking notes, calling a trusted friend or accountability buddy in whom you can confide, or brain dumping your latest and greatest ideas to a utility player on your team, just take care of it and put it aside. Then go into the next situation clean. Meetings should be about driving for an outcome and next step. If you don't leave a meeting moving forward, then all you've done is had a nice chat.

Future Pacing: Staying a Step Ahead of Yourself

An essential quality of leadership is the ability to see the future and design your approach in a manner that will take full advantage of the future envisioned. This means proactive guidance and initiating action as opposed to reacting to whatever occurs. A leader is in front of the situation, not catching up to it, and anticipating, so that surprises don't drop out of nowhere. As a leader it's your responsibility to look at both current events and future possibilities. If you are investing in a specific sector, you need to lead your team toward the trends and currents of that sector. If you are buying real estate in a certain geographic area, you should know the future of that area. If you are directly building a business or investing in a company, you should know the outlook for competition and growth. One example of future pacing, such as in your real estate investments, would work like this:

1. Quantify your target cash flow in precise dollars in a given, future year.
2. Look at the past trends and future indicators for the markets in which your properties are located.
3. Correlate these trends against your current strategies and verify the probability of their effectiveness.
   - Adjust your strategies against these probabilities.
   - Emphasize and support the tactics that will support these strategies.
   - Continue to cull the best franchise players to help you create, develop, and execute your strategies and the best utility players to implement the tactics that will accomplish the strategies.

No one will ever do it like you can do it, but there is not enough of you, or anyone, to go around when so much is going on. A good leader engages the energies and efforts of others to make his or her vision come true, while helping them to do the same. The Wealth Cycle Process requires you to lead your wealth. Let's make sure your brain isn't going to keep you from doing that.

*Running into
your psychology . . .*

13

CONDITIONING
A New Conversation

As you begin the Wealth Cycle Process you will see that your action gets caught up by your belief system. The conversation goes something like this:

"I'm going to be wealthy," says your conscious mind.

"You?" says your subconscious. "No, you're not, you big liar."

At least that's what my brain used to do.

Your beliefs operate on two levels: the conscious, intellectual level and the subconscious, preconditioned level. It's important to understand that any limit to your thinking exists only in the paradigms ingrained in you, not in your potential or your ability to create a big vision. I encourage you to establish a vision that's unencumbered by your paradigms. You created your current financial situation based on your beliefs. As you change your financial situation, this will reprogram your brain to a new, progressive set of beliefs. Unlike processes that suggest you should think your way into thinking, the Be ➡ Do sequence, we believe that you should reprogram your brain the way it was programmed in the first place, by letting it learn from your behavior, a Do ➡ Be sequence. It took you years to be conditioned the way you are, and that conditioning did not come from lectures and thought exercises; it came from behavior and practices. And behavior will turn your brain around. In the Wealth Cycle Process you will act the way you hope to be, and let your brain catch up later.

As I mentioned, I grew up on a farm in Nebraska. My family had always worked hard for their money, and as a result, I always equated working hard with making money, with no idea that my beliefs could not have been further from truth. As I educated myself on human behavior and financial strategies, I learned that it's actually the people who make their money work hard for them, rather than the people who work hard for their money, who end up with more of it. Since creating my millionaire-making program, I've learned that I was not alone. There are many people who shared this same myth.

Much like our views about many things—people, relationships, food, and health to name a few—our beliefs came from our parents, our teachers, and other adults in our lives. And it goes back even further, beyond them, back to the circumstances through which they lived, or what they learned from their parents, what their parents learned from their parents, and so on. These beliefs are ingrained, and because they're usually subconscious, the cycles are continuous—until someone breaks them. You can break the cycle. Beliefs about money are many and varied, but in my research, I've discovered that there are a few that predominate.

MONEY IS SCARCE. Several of us have parents or grandparents who lived through the Great Depression, an era that rooted an entire generation in a scarcity mindset. These people passed onto their children the idea that money was in short supply and that when it did surface, spending had to be limited and saving was imperative. If any of the following ever crossed your mind—"A penny saved is a penny earned," "Don't dip into savings," or "We can't afford it"—then you have this perspective and rainy days loom ominously. Money doesn't grow on trees. These threats create a fearful relationship with money.

MONEY IS EVIL, DIRTY, OR BAD. Several of us have parents or grandparents who believe that the road to bad places is lined with green. They've only ever seen the drawbacks of the rat race, the downside of the money chase, and the audacity and indulgence of those with too much money. Some even believe that wealthy people are bad people. Novels and films often highlight the idea that it's the crooked ones who make the money. The meek shall inherit the earth. Such prophecies create a hands-off relationship with money.

MONEY COMES MONTHLY. The most common way to make a living is to be employed, either with a company or as a skilled professional, with a weekly wage or an annual salary. Historically, this provided the safe, sure thing required by heads of households. Yet, that level of risk was usually balanced with an equal level of reward—low and low. For most, even those who do very well, working for a company or as a skilled professional is a constrained opportunity. Except for the outrageous exceptions, the average CEO of the average company making six figures a year will still experience only a small increase in salary during his or her lifetime. *Slow and steady wins the race.* Such fables create a cautious relationship to money.

MONEY IS NOT FOR ME. Some people feel that they don't deserve to be wealthy or that there is only so much of the millionaire pie to go around. Creating wealth and financial freedom is available to everyone. It is our right to be wealthy, and my hope is that people take their space and know they deserve it. By making money, you are not taking it from someone else; this isn't Bonnie and Clyde Go to the Bank. By making money, you create a greater capacity to contribute, and it's your duty to do this. *Better them than me.* Such adages create a defeated relationship to money.

MONEY IS A MAN THING. There was a time that men made and managed the household money. That time was not so long ago, and some of you may have grown up with such conditioning. Though there are gender tendencies, for example, men tend to carry more money in their pocket than women and are more likely to invest than women, the reasons behind this are not genetic; they are realities falsely fabricated from years of conditioning. Women and men need to understand that money knows no gender. One of my programs that really resonates with up and coming wealth builders is "Wealth Diva: A Man Is Not a Plan." This is a must-do seminar for every man and woman, and the daughters and sons they love. *Let him bring home the bacon.* Such perceptions create an apathetic relationship to money.

MONEY IS GOOD MEDICINE. For some people, retail therapy goes a long way; there's no difficulty a new blouse can't cure. At the moment, we live in a culture of consumerism, and many of us use money to fill the unsatisfying holes in our lives. Some people grew up with a sense of entitlement about money, assuming their parents or a trust fund would always pay for everything, and in the process, they became careless about what they had. This is a vicious and unproductive cycle. The new car gets old, the closet fills up with clothes, and the toys pile up in the playroom. This is not to say there aren't wonderful things to buy and spend our money on; after all, money should be fun. But as with overeating, too much spending on the wrong things can get any of us feeling sluggish and sad. *Shop till you drop.* Such bombarding messages create a disrespectful or nonchalant relationship to money.

MONEY IS ALWAYS A MENACE. For too many of us, money was always a problem. Bills were a hassle, keeping up with the Joneses was exhausting, entrepreneurs were considered nuts, and one's station in life was, well, stationary. And getting rich would be worse. Money can be such a burden, not to mention all that paperwork and responsibility. These views of money create a perspective that money is actually a problem, not a solution. *It's hard enough just to survive, let alone thrive.* Such pessimism creates a negative relationship to money.

MONEY TALK IS TABOO. Many of us have been brought up to believe that conversations about money are in bad taste. Money and financial success, and failures, are considered personal subjects that shouldn't be discussed and certainly shouldn't be taught. Few of us asked our parents how much money they made, and even now, there are people who don't know their spouse's salaries. The results have unintended consequences and have created a world where very few people are having real conversations about money and finances, the very conversations they need to learn and succeed. *These things are not discussed in polite society, dear.* Such a scolding creates an ignorant relationship to money.

In each of these examples, it's clear that unless your parents made a conscious choice to think and act differently, they conditioned you to have the same mindset as them. If you make a decision to break this cycle, you will have the opportunity to teach your children to have more productive beliefs about, and a more profitable relationship to, money. As you come to understand the beliefs you hold, you will work to change them. Through the action steps in this process, and with the help of mentors and respected friends, you will change your behavior. By sharing your desire for new beliefs and asking your mentors and respected friends to help you spot the subconscious limitations you may be putting on yourself, you will teach your brain to follow your behavior. Begin now by restating your beliefs. For example, if you've discovered that you hold any of the above examples as beliefs, you will

1. Change "money is scarce" to "money is abundant" and support a courageous relationship to money.
2. Change "money is evil, dirty, or bad" to "money is good and acceptable" and create a hands-on relationship to money.
3. Change "money comes monthly" to "money comes from a range of sources" and create an opportunistic relationship to money.
4. Change "money is not for me" to "who better than me for money to come to" and create an empowered relationship to money.
5. Change "money is a man thing" to "I can and will know about and understand money," and create a thoughtful relationship to money.
6. Change "money is good medicine" to "money is a tool to help make my life better" and create a respectful and concerned relationship to money.
7. Change "money is a menace" to "money is a solution" and create a positive relationship to money.
8. Change "money talk is taboo" to "money talk is vital" and create a knowledgeable relationship to money.

You can see how much better it is to be courageous, hands-on, opportunistic, empowered, thoughtful, respectful and concerned, positive, and knowledgeable than to be fearful, hands-off, cautious, defeated, apathetic, disrespectful and nonchalant, negative, and ignorant. The choice is yours and it looks like you're well on your way. You've already taken a huge step by deciding to actually take the first step. By making the decision to start right now, you have created the opportunity to raise your financial consciousness and change your life.

Self-Fulfilling Prophecies

Looking deeply into your beliefs is an important start to changing your behavior. As you go through these exercises, there are a wide range of responses you may have, from simply thinking they are stupid, to becoming physically ill. Your beliefs are buried deep at the cellular level, so of course, as you attempt to restate your new ones, every cell in your body may revolt against you. I recommend that you face each of these challenges as a reinforcement of the fact that this is progress, and what you are doing is right.

Assess Your Mindset

Finish and reflect on this statement: "Money is . . ." Consider the beliefs stated above, and see if any resonate with you. Money is . . . scarce, evil, bad or dirty, comes only monthly, a man thing, medicine, menacing or taboo. Or perhaps for you it's something else altogether. Try to remember what your conditioning may have been. This will help you to either change it if it was negative or reinforce it if it was positive.

It is very important, during this stage, that you do not get side-tracked by judging the people who raised you. There is no doubt they had your best interests at heart and did the best they could, most likely having learned it from a culture that dictated commonly held and subconsciously acknowledged agreements about money.

After you've done this assessment you need to take this very important action step. Conduct a three-month review of your calendar and checkbook. If you ever want to see what a person is truly committed to, these are the sources. Look for themes and patterns of spending time and money. Most likely, your day-to-day activities and spending are a result of the way you think. Once thinking changes, so will the results of this review of your activities and spending.

Blast through Barriers

Reconsider the phrases in your brain. Play to win, not to lose. Be decisive, not tentative. Increase and expand your money, rather than holding onto, preserving, and protecting it. Be excited and enthusiastic, not fearful or overly cautious. Wealthy people are proactive and create the lives they want to live. Consider your language. The vocabulary you choose not only reflects, but actually affects, your thinking. For example, the word *if* is conditional, the word *when* is definitive. From this point on, your dreams and goals are when, not if. Do not let if pass your lips in relation to this pursuit. You will get there, there's no doubt—it's only a matter of when. Begin now, "When I become a millionaire, I will . . ." Similarly, try saying yes, not no, to what you will and can do.

You must reset your mind and psychology to reinforce what it is you want, instead of supporting the very thing from which you would like to move away. You can start by restating your beliefs to reverse that financial conditioning. Take the statements you've summarized about the preconceived notions you culled from childhood, such as "Money is difficult to earn and even more difficult to keep," and flip that around. In this example, that would restate to "Money comes freely to me; money is easy to keep and multiply."

It may seem trite, but it's anything but. Experts will support the fact that something tangible occurs when you, and others, hear you verbalize your beliefs. While you restate your beliefs you are announcing your dreams to yourself, which is the first step in making those dreams come true. And when others hear your dream, loud and clear, they begin to understand the real you better, and can help direct you, through referrals, resources, and so on, toward your goal. It's a prosperous cycle and it starts with you, what you believe and, as importantly, what you say.

Conceive a New Perspective

Most people do not have a clear direction or vision of what they want their life to look like when they have great wealth. Though no official ceremony takes place, too many people have said "I do" to their current reality, making a lifetime commitment to something that really doesn't satisfy. This is an opportunity for you to clarify your purpose and create a vision and step forward toward making it happen.

The financial gap from where you are to where you want to be should be a doable trek, and the top of that Gap Analysis should provide the motivation to commit to generating wealth.

Money Muscles

You all have money muscles—they're just atrophied little guys. If you had a dream to run a marathon, your first steps would most likely be to get some running shoes, stretch out the kinks, and jog a few miles. Similarly, if you dream of being a millionaire, you need to start with the building blocks that will help you go the distance. Becoming a millionaire requires getting into financial shape, and that means building your money muscles. Many of us are obsessed with our health and fitness, prompted by the media, consumer product companies, and the entertainment world. It's also pervaded our conversation, sparked by articles and journals, making us proficient in fitness studies, diets, medical procedures, and scientific terminology. People have no problem revealing the most intimate details of their health to perfect strangers.

As health and fitness govern our physical lives, money and finances affect our economic lives. Money may not be the most important thing in life, but I'm pretty sure it can have the most impact. Whether right or wrong, it seems that more people measure themselves by the yardstick of their wealth than by their health, and yet money and finance conversations are rarely had. If the conversation does occur, it usually covers general issues like Wall Street or the nation's credit card debt, not anything personal or specific, like our own portfolio or bad debt.

If you want to become a millionaire, it's time to get in shape, to build the money muscles, and run the race toward wealth. As with all exercise programs, the first days are the most difficult; you'll be a little sore at first. Not only will it take your brain a while to adjust to this new behavior of focusing on your finances and committing to a positive perception of money, but it will also require a time commitment. This means that you will have to build this program into your schedule. This too, will seem second nature after a while. Kind of like taking an hour to jog, or to watch a favorite TV show, or meditate. As those things eventually fit into your day, so will this, and it will make each day of your life more important and significant. Time and again, I see that when I put substance into my schedule, the unsubstantial moves off. As you progress, and you get financially conditioned, it will become more fun and exciting, and it will get easier and easier. You won't believe you've not been doing it your entire life.

Financial Consciousness

In order to sustain the new financial consciousness that will support your vision, you need to realize a few of the landmines that are going to threaten your progress. Knowing that they are there is more than half the battle.

1. The little voice in your head is going to mess with your plan. There's no getting around it; there is a lot of noise in your brain. The ingredients that make up this recipe of noise include excuses, blaming, confusion, disjointed conversations, rationalizing, procrastinating, distraction, and lack of focus. They need no introduction and no explanation—we know them all too well. As you move forward you turn off the noise of your brain.

2. Perception of your behavior and your actual behavior are not necessarily, and most likely are not, the same. The dichotomy between our conscious selves and our subconscious selves undermines what you think you believe and what your behavior would indicate you believe. Once you start saying your belief out loud, the incongruity will become more obvious to both you and others and your behavior will start to line up.

3. You may get stuck in your own story. The stories we contrive in our heads started with the results we observed, usually those of adults around us, and continue with the results we create, usually very similar to the ones we observed as kids. This is a vicious cycle. Our story is created from our experiences. Each time we have an

experience, we filter that through our feeling and reason, to either confirm or deny the truths we believe. For example, if you invest in a real estate deal and it fails and you lose your money, you can choose either to learn from the experience, by taking the lesson and building a new experience, or to get stuck in the drama of your story.

I had a client who got so much satisfaction out of being stuck in her story that she preferred to fail rather than prove her story wrong. She was what I call a seminar junkie, constantly seeking out information to affirm her fears. She had a nest egg of about $30,000, and though she had a desire to build a business, she was going to do all she could to keep that nest egg safe and sound, even if that meant smothering it to death in savings and careful spending. Her reasoning behind this behavior was rational, and I'd seen it so often I understood it well. She'd worked so hard for that money, and had so much pain associated with its accumulation, that she would never let anyone take it away from her. Her relationship to money was definitely cautious and fearful, yet she had a desire to create great wealth. Her story and her psyche were clearly out of sync.

After too many unsuccessful attempts to get her to put her $30,000 into wealth-generating assets, I moved off that strategy and focused on improving her Cash Machine. But after some small effort, she stopped following any of the revenue-generating marketing and sales strategies we'd laid out, and nine months in, she declared that I wasn't doing anything for her.

That was the final clue I needed to realize that this problem would not be solved through strategies and suggestions. Wealthy people do the work. No one will play your game for you; you have to play your own game. It was time for straight talk.

"Let me tell you what you didn't do for you," I said. "You wouldn't make a decision, you wouldn't follow anyone's advice, we wrote up a marketing plan and you didn't follow any of the action steps on it, you didn't follow up on any of the networking connections we established, nor did you pursue any of the specific markets we'd segmented and targeted. Who is it that is doing nothing for you?"

The plan didn't need to change; she needed to recommit to it. Finally, she did. She followed the new pricing and positioning strategy we'd outlined in her marketing strategy. She aggressively networked and went after new markets. And most important, she did all this with the belief that she would succeed, rather than with her old motivation of proving the world wrong. Finally, she got unstuck from her story.

If you do not recognize your truths, you will continue to affirm negative truths. I often tell my clients "Don't get stuck; get it done." If you have stated new truths, then you can reflect on each experience in a new light and spiral up into a better story. A self-fulfilling prophecy is better when the prophecy is positive.

4. Nonexistent competition may seem overwhelming. News flash: There's enough for everyone. If you find you are fighting with everyone else over the same piece of pie instead of making the pie bigger, then you are with the wrong group of people in the wrong game. Replace competition with creation and bring balance into your life.

5. Visions are easier said than done. Ask anyone who studies leadership the number one quality of a leader and they will tell you it's having a vision. Having a vision takes courage, and staying power, and commitment. It also requires that the person with the vision have a good team around him or her, such as a supportive spouse or partner, understanding and involved children, and experts, such as mentors, lawyers, and bookkeepers, who will play their proper position and play it well.

6. Quitting on the vision might be easier. Stasis and inertia are always easier choices than change. But just when you do think of

quitting, remember this: according to actuary tables published by the insurance industry, people whose only goal is to reach a certain age and just retire, without a bigger vision of what that financial freedom looks like, pass away within two years of reaching that milestone. These people haven't bothered to plan their life beyond that point, and that life disappears. If they had made the choice you're making and opted for a bigger vision and financial freedom, they could have made all their dreams come true.

The vision is yours. The journey is yours. The team you build around you to take the journey and the action you take to achieve the vision are all yours. You must be willing to be the leader of your own life if you want to make yourself a millionaire.

The Wealth Cycle Process is a nonnegotiable commitment to action, and it's okay if you don't believe the restated conditioning before you begin. As I've said, I believe that it takes action to reconstruct and then reinforce thought and that those who do it the opposite way, waiting for the belief in order to create the action, have a long wait. By acting first, the reaction is visceral, as it was when the notions were first imbedded. This will create a more enduring change, because you're not painting over old paint, but stripping the walls and starting over. You will be uncomfortable, and maybe even frustrated, but that's because you're growing. The action begins.

My Vision

My son Logan and I were driving up to our lake house when the television producer called. "Loral," she said. "We want to do financial makeovers."

"Do I have déjà vu or do you?"

"We want to do a regular series," she said. "You take randomly selected individuals and make them millionaires."

"That sounds good," I said.

"Did you hear what I said?"

" 'You want to take randomly selected individuals and make them millionaires.' "

"Right," she said. "We'll pick anyone from anywhere and you'll make them wealthy. On TV."

"And?"

"And, you haven't hung up on me."

"Should I?" I asked.

"Do you think you can do it?" the producer asked.

"I know I can," I said. I turned north toward the state line.

"I know you can too," she said.

Passing on the
Legacy of Wealth . . .

14

TEACH YOUR CHILDREN
Doing It Differently for the Next Generation

One day, after a seminar in Houston, my son, Logan, who is 5 years old and works for the company as a model, was watching diligently as we were packing up a Team-Made Millionaire event. Trying to help, Logan was right at the leg of one of our team members. Finally, the team member decided there was a task he could give my son. He asked Logan to count all the chairs in the room and report back with a final tally. Less than 30 seconds later, fingers tugged at his shorts. Logan had returned. "Give up?" the team member asked.

"No," Logan said. "I know the number."

The team member cocked his eyebrow. "That's impossible," he said.

"Twelve hundred and forty-eight."

"That's a guess, right?" the team member said, but Logan shook his head. Before I could jump to the conclusion that Jodi Foster was going to play me in some wacky movie about a kid genius, Logan pointed to the hotel staffer stacking chairs.

"I asked him how many chairs were in the room, and he told me," Logan said.

Level three listening, sequencing, and self-management. And he's 5.

Starting Young

This type of leadership and teamwork thinking can be, and should be, taught young. Not only is my son an active part of my business, but he knows what we do at my company, Live Out Loud, and with our Team-Made Millionaires. He knows about my investment projects, goes on business trips with me, has a Wealth Account and even a Roth IRA. And though I can more than afford to grant every wish his big heart desires, he does not receive anything until he's earned the money to pay for half of it, and then he must continue earning the rest or it's put on hold until he does. He's never heard me say we can't afford something and he knows that we lead our wealth by keeping the money we make ahead of the money we spend. He also understands that we invest directly in assets, ("Mom, are people going to pay us to live in these houses too?") and have to create a Cash Machine to fuel those assets ("Can I help sign books at the Team-Made Millionaire seminar this weekend?" On a side note, maybe it's just a mom talking, but that autograph will be worth something someday.)

Members of our Team-Made Millionaire community are currently teaching the ideas of the Wealth Cycle to grade school, high school, and college students. The great discovery is that the students are not nearly as uncomfortable or uneasy about the Wealth Cycle Process as some adults seem to be. Not only are they eager for this type of information—in fact, three-quarters of high school students surveyed stated they'd like a finance or wealth class in school, but they have a ready capacity to absorb it because they are not yet that deep into the Lifestyle Cycles that holds back most of their parents.

We must do money differently for the next generation. It's time to teach financial literacy to our children. Since the education system doesn't offer financial literacy programs, the responsibility of developing their financial knowledge is on you. Wealth building and healthy, out-loud relationships to money can be ingrained as early as infancy, and I encourage you as a parent, grandparent, aunt, uncle, guardian, or teacher to begin now to educate the children in your life on wealth building. Just imagine how wonderful a gift that would have been if someone had extended the wisdom of how to build wealth to you.

Giving to Get

Philanthropy starts early. As important as it is to teach a child the building blocks of the Wealth Cycle—to invest, to stay out of debt, to make money with money and create a Cash Machine using one's skills—it's also important to teach charity. It is part of my son's annual Christmas routine to choose five of his toys and give them away to an organization that can give them to children in need. I also encourage setting aside a percentage of a child's earnings, even if it's from a lemonade stand, to go to worthwhile causes. Benevolent habits can and should be imbedded early.

Financial Literacy

I believe we can break the cycle of financial illiteracy in a number of ways.

1. Establish a wealth account for each child when that child is born.

2. Teach children, at an early age, to put a fixed percentage of their allowance or gifts, and later earnings from part-time jobs, into their Wealth Accounts. Even if the child only gets a small gift once in a while, have them deposit as much as 50 percent of it into the Wealth Account.

3. Motivate them and reinforce their new habit by periodically showing them how much their Wealth Account has grown.

4. Share positive financial information so that they can see the possibility of abundance. Never say you can't afford something. You can still be direct, without being negative. Make a plan to get creative about making money.

5. Share the realities of business. If your child's lemonade stand sold $10 of lemonade that cost $12 to make, you need to explain that, although they had fun, they did not make a profit. Help them figure out how to do it differently, and more profitably, the next time.

6. Establish money days, for example, the first Monday of every month, where you share what you've learned in this process.

7. Show and teach leadership by asking your children open-ended questions about their schedules and plans so they learn the value of sequencing, decisive thinking, and communication.

8. Encourage your children to always give a percentage of their earnings to charity and good causes.

This is a parental duty and inheritance. Showing your children how to form lifelong patterns will enable them to live prosperously and enjoy a healthy relationship to money. Time and again, the people who we've coached tell us that they are thrilled to learn that it is actually possible to veer off their unsatisfying track and generate wealth with much less difficulty than they ever imagined. Mostly, though, they can't believe that no one taught them these simple truths about wealth a long time ago. Talking out loud with your children about wealth and money is the best inheritance you can give them.

EPILOGUE

Are You Willing to Create and Execute the Wealth Cycle Process?

The eighth question of the Gap Analysis is: "Are you willing to create and execute the Wealth Cycle process?" I want my clients to say yes and take massive action.

My personal vision is to expand the business we have at Live Out Loud until it's a global education house. My colleagues and I bootstrapped our way to develop this community, a community that values the ideal that we give to get, and we hope to help others do the same. It's about wrapping our wealth knowledge around more and more people until we've turned this nation on its brain and created a country of millionaires. Look how great we would be if we all started to live conscious lives. We know this country is capable of mass movement because we somehow became a country of consumers. Let's turn that capacity around and move in a productive direction.

Since these ideas will strike each person differently, everyone is going to do it differently, and my colleagues and I encourage that. You must play the game you want to play, a game that fits into your values and works with what you ultimately want. While our community of wealth is all about collaboration and teamwork, there's no dependency. We like healthy, responsible relationships. We each have to write our own script, follow our own sequence of Wealth Cycle building blocks, and create our own plan. It's you who needs to decide that you should get what you want. Take on that role like you're a wealth warrior. Get in front of your situation and make this process work for you. There is plenty of abundance; it's a ripoff for you not to do this. A wealth builder is just someone who's awake and wants to have an out-loud conversation, that is, a conscious, thoughtful life. It's time to run headlong into your fears and make them disappear.

If you want something new, you must do something different today. There's no finish line to this pursuit; you should always be planning for what's possible. Diligence, planning, knowing what you want—these are what it takes to get to a better place. Opportunities swirl around this planet constantly. I'm sure that if each of us felt we deserved the best, we would believe more in ourselves, and in others, and in all that's out there to share, and we would reach out for a handful of that opportunity.

Say yes. Stand up for yourself, live out loud, and be accountable. You do deserve that opportunity. Now you're ready to plan for what is possible and propel yourself toward a future of financial freedom and wealth.

RESOURCES

I have found the following references and resources helpful:

BUSINESS AND ENTREPRENEURSHIP

The E-Myth: Why Most Businesses Don't Work and What To Do About It, Michael Gerber

Innovation and Entrepreneurship, Peter F. Drucker

Harvard Business Review on Entrepreneurship, Harvard Business Review

The Portable MBA in Entrepreneurship, William D. Bygrave and Andrew Zacharakis

The Ewing Marion Kauffman Foundation of Entrepreneurship, www.kauffman.org

TAXES

Lower Your Taxes—Big Time!:

Wealth Building, Tax Reduction Secrets from an IRS Insider, Sandy Botkin

WEALTH BUILDING AND FIANACE

Think and Grow Rich, Napoleon Hill

Multiple Streams Of Income, Robert G. Allen

The Millionaire Next Door: The Surprising Secrets of America's Wealthy, Thomas J. Stanley and William D. Danko

In addition, you can get help from my team by emailing teammademillionaire@liveoutloud.com or email me directly at TheMillionaireMaker@liveoutloud.com, and I can refer you to help and information on

Debt Elimination Support And Plans
Entities
Forecasting And Expense Management
Home Equity Strategies
Iras
Mortgage Solutions
Wealth Accounts

INDEX

About the Author

Loral Langemeier is a master coach, financial strategist, and multimillionaire who reaches many thousands of individuals each year. She is the founder of Live Out Loud, a coaching and seminar company that teaches her trademarked Wealth Cycle program one person at a time.

Free Tickets to See Loral Live!

To get two free tickets to an upcoming
Team Made Millionaire event in your city, go to
www.themillionairemakerbook.com today!*

ACT NOW—SEATING IS LIMITED

Use VIP code MCG-106MMBK when requesting your free tickets.

*For upcoming dates and locations for this international seminar, or to reserve your complimentary seats,
call 1-888-262-2402, email info@liveoutloud.com, or visit www.themillionairemakerbook.com.